Hamlet 2020

A play in 5 acts by
William Shakespeare
&
Mick Theebs

Copyright © 2020 by Mick Theebs, LLC

ISBN: 978-1-7325503-1-5

Greenwich, CT

June 1, 2020

All rights reserved. This book or any portion thereof may not be reproduced or used in any manner whatsoever without the express written permission of the author except for the use of brief quotations in a book review or scholarly journal.

History repeats itself first as tragedy, second as farce

-Karl Marx

For America.

Special Thanks

I would like to take a moment to thank all of the people who made this book possible. Thank you to Taylor Rajaniemi and Keith Roland for your notes and copyediting, this book would not be half as funny without your expert advice. Thank you to The Written Word Milford Writer's Group for providing me with a community of support and enthusiasm. Thank you to my wife-to-be and all of my other friends and family who have provided me with love and encouragement. Thank you to William Shakespeare for writing one of the greatest pieces of English literature ever written and thank you in advance to his descendents for hopefully having a sense of humor about his work. And finally thank you, the reader.

-Mick Theebs
May 24, 2020

Prologue

Note: Whoever is directing this play is encouraged to write their own speech to be given before the performance.

Spotlight in front of closed curtain.

Writer: What you are about to watch is a bastardization of one of the greatest pieces of literature ever written by human hand. All the beautiful poetry of the original writer's lines has been stripped away and replaced by dirty words and lewd jokes to suit our modern times. While the original plot has been preserved, many aspects have been "updated" in order to more be relevant to our unique point in history. This is not high art, so if you were expecting a night of class and elegance, you are going to be sorely disappointed. Rather, this play is keeping in the grand tradition of the theatre, that is, it is entertainment for the masses. With that being said, I present to you all Hamlet 2020.

Act I

You Look Like You've Seen a Ghost

Scene I

Outside the Castle Gates.
Francisco, the nearsighted watchman, stands at his post.

Bernardo enters from the gate

Bernardo: Is anybody home?

Francisco: Halt, who goes there?

Bernardo: C'mon, man, you know it's me.

Francisco: Hmm...Bernardo?

Bernardo (*annoyed*): Yeah, dude. You need to get your ass to the eye doctor...

Francisco: It's about time you got here.

Bernardo: My shift doesn't start until midnight, so I get here at midnight. You got a problem with it, take it up with the new king.

Francisco: Whatever. He's busy enough in his warm bed with the queen, while I'm freezing my nuts off out here.

Bernardo: Cry me a river. Anything interesting happen tonight?

Francisco: Nothin' crazy. I wrote my name in the snow earlier. (*starts to leave*) Welp, I'm off. That whiskey ain't going to drink itself.

Bernardo: Impressive stuff. Have one for me, will ya? Oh, and if you see Horatio and Marcellus on your way out, tell them to hurry up.

Francisco: I think someone is coming right now. (*Looks off in the*

I.I

(Francisco cont.)
distance) Halt! Who goes there?

Enter Horatio and Marcellus

Horatio: Who do you think?

Marcellus: You really need to get your eyes looked at Francisco, you're blind as a goddamned bat.

Francisco: All right, I'm off the clock. I don't need to stand around and take this in the cold.

Marcellus: You're off the clock? Who's your replacement?

Francisco (*pointing at Bernardo*): Direct all queries to Colonel Limpdick over there. I'm gonna go get drunk now. Goodnight ladies.

Francisco Exits

Marcellus (*to Bernardo*): When did you get promoted to Colonel?

Bernardo: It was right after I finished ringing your mom's bell. I see you brought Horatio with you.

Horatio: Yeah, I'm here in spite of my better judgment. I can't believe you drunk idiots convinced me to come out here in the freezing cold in the middle of the night.

Marcellus: Horatio here is a skeptic, says he "doesn't believe in ghosts." Have you seen anything so far?

Bernardo: My shift just started, so no.

Marcellus: Well, we've seen this thing twice now and some of us were sober when it happened. Horatio thinks he's so goddamned

I.I

(Marcellus cont.)
smart, so I said to him "come on and see for yourself. If you're so sure, I'll bet you twenty bucks you'll see the ghost tonight."

Horatio (*shivering*): And I gotta say, I'm starting to question if this is even worth the easy twenty bucks.

Bernardo: I don't know how easy that money is gonna be, Horatio. We've all seen the ghost two nights in a row now...

Horatio: Ah, don't tell me you believe in this ghost stuff, too.

Bernardo: I believe what I see and what I saw was a ghost. It came around the same time each night. Between midnight and one. So, we should see it any minute...

Marcellus: Oh shit, look! There it is!

Enter Ghost

Bernardo: Kinda looks like the old king, doesn't it? You see what I'm talking about Horatio?

Horatio (*squinting*): It is wearing the king's old armor. But that could be anyone. How do I know you didn't dress Francisco up to mess with me?

Marcellus (*grinning*): Ask him for yourself.

Horatio: Francisco? Is that you? This ain't funny, you blind bastard. Say something!

Ghost starts to walk away.

Marcellus: Looks like you pissed it off.

Bernardo: And there it goes...

I.I

Horatio (*shouting at ghost's back*): Say something!

Exit Ghost

Marcellus: It's gone and it ain't saying nothing.

Bernardo (*smirking*): What's the matter, Horatio? You look like you've seen a ghost!

Horatio (*shaken*): That...wasn't Francisco?

Marcellus: It looked like the dead king, didn't it?

Horatio: Definitely. He was wearing the same armor he wore when we beat Norway in the war. Crazy stuff.

Marcellus holds out his hand to Horatio and clears his throat.

Horatio: Yeah, yeah. Here's your twenty. (*Places money in Marcellus' hand*) Jesus. I've got a bad feeling about this ghost.

Marcellus (*pocketing money*): Now that that's settled, lemme ask you a question, smart-guy. Why do you got everyone working so hard making cannons and building ships? My brother hasn't had a day off in almost a month. Something's up and I gotta feeling you know something the rest of us don't.

Horatio (*sighs*): I probably shouldn't be telling you this, but we're preparing for an attack from Norway. You know, we beat them in the war a few years ago and took some land from them. And with our old king dead and the new one just sworn in, everyone up top is worried that the son of the king we crushed is gonna try to catch us with our pants down.

Bernardo: You think maybe this ghost is a sign that Norway is going to attack us, since it's wearing the same armor?

I.I

Horatio: Maybe. All I know is that I got a bad feeling about the future of Denmark. It makes me think of the stories I heard about Rome the night before Caesar was killed. They say the dead were stirring in their graves, rolling over in their sleep. They were also saying that the stars were falling from the sky and- oh shit here it comes again!

Enter Ghost

Horatio: Hey! Wait! You're back? Stop! We wanna talk to you! Do you know something? Do you have a warning from the other side? Are you guarding your buried treasure? By all that is holy, I command you, speak! Say something, goddamn it!

Rooster crows

Horatio: Do something, Marcellus!

Marcellus (*drawing sword*): ...Should I try to stab it?

Horatio (*drawing sword*): Whatever it takes to keep it from leaving!

Marcellus (*swinging sword*): Take that!

Horatio (*swinging sword*): And one of these!

Exit Ghost

Marcellus: It's gone. In retrospect, we probably shouldn't have tried to kill the ghost.

Bernardo: It looked like it was about to say something before the rooster crowed.

Horatio: And then it left. I heard somewhere that ghosts don't like the sound of roosters. They're allergic.

I.I

Marcellus (*stares at Horatio*): Where the hell did you hear that?

Horatio: I don't know, I read it in a book somewhere. It doesn't matter. What we need to do is tell Hamlet about this ghost. Since it looks like his dead dad, it might talk to him.

Marcellus: All right. It's worth a shot. I think I know where we can find him, too.

Horatio and Marcellus exit.

Bernardo: No, that's cool, just leave without saying goodbye.

Scene II

King's Throne Room. It is covered in gaudy gold leaf, marble, and crystal. It basically looks like a hotel lobby. The King and Queen sit on their thrones. Hamlet, Polonius, Laertes, and Diplomats are all standing around.

King: As everybody knows, it's a real shame that my brother died so suddenly and under such mysterious circumstances. The entire country is saddened about the old king passing away, especially when he was so healthy and strong and definitely not in poor health at all. But even in this time of pain and sorrow, let's all appreciate the fact that the queen, my sister-in-law, was able to forget the grief of the sudden and mysterious passing of her husband, my brother, long enough to marry me, Claudius, and make me the new king only a few weeks after his passing. And it's a good thing that we now have a strong leader at the helm because the word is that Fortinbras the Norwegian is supposedly sending agents into our country. They're bringing drugs. They're bringing crime. Now, let's call it what it is, folks. This is Radical Norwegian Terrorism and I'm the only one who can stop it. Which is why I'm sending two of our smartest diplomats to Norway. We've got the best diplomats here in Denmark, don't we folks? They're going to leave to speak with Fortinbras today and let them know that if this Radical Norwegian Terrorism doesn't end, we will have to show them what the strongest army in the world can do by bringing them fire and fury!

Diplomat: You mean right now? We aren't fully prepared to leave yet and we haven't received all the intel on Norway...

King: I said go!

Diplomat: Yes sir! (*mumbling as they leave*)...Idiot.

Exit Diplomat

I.II

King: Okay, next order of business. Laertes! You said you had something you wanted to ask me earlier. Your father has been a great friend to the throne, so anything you want, just name it and it's yours. What'll it be?

Laertes: Your grace, as you already know, I attended school in France. I had a lot of fun out there. Like, a lot of fun. I gotta say, I'm missing it... (*pauses for a beat as he reflects on his memories of France, then remembers himself*) ...So I was wondering if I could have your permission to return to France for more fun.

King: Did you ask your father's permission?

Polonius: Yes, my liege. He wore me down and I finally told him yes, having remembered my own days of frolicking with the French maids. Why, I remember this one time with this one girl, she was a milkmaid, or was she a seamstress? In any case, she was a maid with unconventional tastes. In fact, she was the one who first introduced me to the wonderful novelty of "pegging"...

King: Get to the point, Polonius.

Polonius: Oh, yes. I told my son that it was fine so long as you agreed.

King: Sure, fine, whatever. Knock yourself out Laertes. Okay, now that's taken care of, let's see how my nephew-slash-number-one-son is doing.

Hamlet (*aside*): Oh god, he's talking to me.

King: Why're you such a Gloomy Gus?

Hamlet: I'm not a Gloomy Gus.

Queen: Maybe we should change your name from Hamlet to Gloomy Gus, since you're so gloomy. I know you're upset about

(Queen Cont.)
your father dying under mysterious circumstances, but you need to move on. People die every day.

Hamlet: That's true.

Queen: If you know it's true, then why are you acting like a Gloomy Gus?

Hamlet: You guys don't even understand the pain that haunts my soul! These black clothes and mascera only show a fraction of the gloominess inside me. You'll never understand!

King: Listen, I know you're sad about your father dying under mysterious circumstances, but you need to get over it. It's been like six weeks. Think about how I feel. You lost your father, but I lost a brother and then I had to take his throne and marry his beautiful widow. People lose their fathers every day and most of them aren't lucky enough to have uncles to marry their moms, so you should count your blessings. Think of me as your new dad. It's what your father would have wanted before his mysterious death. And as for going back to school, your mother and I think it might be best for the family for you to stay with us until you're less gloomy.

Queen: I'm really worried for you, Gus, I mean, Hamlet.

Hamlet: (*sighs*) I guess I don't have a choice, do I?

King: Nope. Anyways, Gertrude, let's go back to the bed you used to share with my brother. I invite everyone into the royal chambers to watch how the new King performs!

Exit All but Hamlet

Hamlet: Gross. God, I hate him so much. He's not even a tenth of the man that my father was. He's gonna run this country straight

I.II

(Hamlet Cont.)
into the ground, I just know it. I wish it wasn't a sin to kill myself, because that's the only way I can see myself getting out of this nightmare. What does my mom even see in him? It hasn't even been two months and she's already hopped into bed with this buffoon. Dad's body probably wasn't even cold when that snake made his move and she fell for it and married him. I wish there was something I could do about all of this. If only there was a sign...

Enter Horatio and Marcellus and Bernardo

Horatio: Hamlet! There you are!

Hamlet: Uh...hey, uh...chief. Good to see you...Horatio?

Horatio: Good to see you, too, my lord.

Hamlet: No need for formalities. I'm a regular guy just like you, except I'm next in line to run the entire country. What are you doing here? Shouldn't you guys be working or something?

Horatio: Meh, we blew it off. Plus, there was your dad's funeral...

Hamlet: I think you mean my Mom's wedding.

Horatio: I mean, it did happen in the same hall fifteen minutes later...

Hamlet (*sarcastic*): Yeah, but think of the savings, Horatio! We didn't have to cater a funeral and a wedding! We had it all at once. (*sadly*) If Dad had been there to see that...

Horatio: Speaking of seeing your dad...

Hamlet: Yeah, it's a real shame I'm never, ever going to see him again.

I.II

Horatio: Yeah, about that, I'm pretty sure I saw him last night.

Hamlet: What?

Horatio: Your dad. The dead king.

Hamlet: You saw my dad? Where?!

Horatio: You're never going to believe it...

Hamlet: Tell me!

Horatio: So, for the past couple nights the guards have been visited by...uh...well, a ghost. And the ghost is wearing your father's armor from the Norwegian wars. I didn't believe it when they told me, and so I went and saw for myself and, I shit you not, there was the ghost of your father.

Marcellus: Don't forget to tell him about the part where you gave me twenty bucks.

Hamlet: Where did you see him?

Marcellus: At the guard tower.

Hamlet: Did you try talking to him?

Horatio: Yeah, but it didn't say anything. Before we could...uh... convince it to talk, the rooster crowed and it left.

Hamlet: Weird.

Horatio: I know it sounds crazy but that's how it went down. We figured you'd want to know about this.

Hamlet: Are you guys holding watch again tonight?

I.II

Bernardo: Uh, yeah. It's our job. We do it literally every single night.

Hamlet: …He was wearing armor?

Marcellus: Yep

Hamlet: His entire body?

Bernardo: That's usually what armor is meant to protect.

Hamlet: So, you didn't see his face, then?

Horatio: He had the visor up, so we did.

Hamlet: Did he look like he missed me?

Horatio: I guess it looked kind of sad.

Hamlet: Was his face red or white?

Horatio: I mean, it was a ghost, so…see through?

Hamlet: Did he look at you?

Horatio: Yeah, it looked right at all of us.

Hamlet: How long did it hang around for?

Horatio: I don't know. I was too busy seeing a ghost to check my watch.

Marcellus: Probably a couple of minutes.

Hamlet: Did he have a beard?

Horatio: Uh…I guess. Does it matter? Look, I'm telling you I saw

I.II

(**Horatio cont.**)
the ghost of your dead father. Let me just reiterate that I saw a goddamn ghost.

Hamlet: Hmm...I guess I will have to find out if he has a beard for myself. I'll join you guys on your watch tonight and see if it comes out again.

Horatio: Seems like there's a good chance it will.

Hamlet: Awesome. And if it's really the ghost of my dad, he'll talk to me and tell me that he loves me and misses me and that he's proud of his little fancy boy...uh...Listen, can you guys do me a favor and not tell anyone about this ghost business? I don't want them to think I'm going crazy or something.

Marcellus: What's our silence worth to you?

Hamlet, grumbling, gives each of them some money.

Marcellus, Bernardo, Horatio: As you wish, my lord!

Hamlet: Yeah, yeah...now can you guys get outta here? I need to do some brooding on this.

Exit Marcellus, Bernardo, Horatio.

Hamlet: Oh man! This might be the sign I was looking for! Papa's ghost! Maybe there was something about his mysterious death that makes it so his spirit can't find peace! I can't wait to find out!

Scene III

Polonius' House. A nice clean house that obviously belongs to a member of the nobility. Decorated in the standard rich person way: big pieces of art, expensive fragile vases sitting on precarious platforms.
Laertes and Ophelia are in the living room. Ophelia sits on a couch while Laertes gathers up his things for his trip.

Laertes: Welp, I'm all packed up to go to France. Don't forget to write me, little sister.

Ophelia: Of course, I will.

Laertes: Oh, and one more thing before I go. Stay away from Hamlet. He's bad news.

Ophelia: He says before going to France to whore it up.

Laertes: And that's why I know better than anyone else. I know how guys think. We're only after one thing. He might say that he cares for you now, but believe me, once he gets what he's after he'll move on to the next tart. And where will that leave you? Nobody wants to marry a girl who's been used up. And I know you're going to say: "Oh, but Hamlet is different. He says he loves me." Do you realize how many girls I've confessed my love to, Ophelia? Thousands. And they all believed it every time. In fact, I'll probably tell hundreds more in France that I love them when I get back there. It's the quickest way into a maid's…uh…heart. (*Clears throat*) Anyways, Hamlet is the heir to the throne and you're just… well, you.

Ophelia: …Yeah, I'll keep that in mind. (rolls eyes) Maybe you should worry more about where you're sticking your junk before you worry about what's going on with mine. Frankly, it's amazing that you haven't caught syphilis and died already.

I.III

Laertes: Oh, don't worry, I've got loads of syphilis- oh shit, here comes Dad, be cool.

Enter Polonius

Laertes: Hey Dad! We were just talking about geopolitics. Welp, I better get going-

Polonius: Ah, where do you think you're going you little scamp? So quick to go to France and prance around with the maids around the May Pole, are you? I'll bet you're interested in having a different kind of pole pranced around! (*chuckles*) In all seriousness, you need to stay out of trouble when you're out there though. There's nothing wrong with raising a little mischief, but make sure to keep it quiet. I can't have you besmirching the proud family legacy. So that means no gambling, no fighting, and no making a fool of yourself. Measure your words carefully before you speak because otherwise you may come off as an ignorant windbag that has no idea what they're talking about. We wouldn't want the name "Bin Laden" associated with anything vulgar or unsavory. If you're going to experiment with the ladies, make sure you pay them all well so that they all keep their mouths shut. I remember this one time I was trying to be appointed to the king's council and this woman came forward saying that I grabbed her by the-

Laertes: Yeah, Dad, that's cool and everything but I'm gonna be late for my boat.

Polonius: All right, well, go on and get out of here you rascal!

Laertes: See you later, sis. Don't forget what I told you.

Ophelia: About Hamlet or about your syphilis?

Laertes (*whispering through grit teeth*): Yo, be cool. (*loudly*) Okay, bye!

I.III

Exit Laertes

Polonius: What was that all about, Ophelia?

Ophelia (*dismissive*): Oh, he was just trying to talk to me about Hamlet.

Polonius: Yes, he's been very concerned about your relationship with the Prince. I must say, I think he's right. You need to watch your step around him, Ophelia. I know right now it seems like he loves you, but I know how fickle men can be. You've got your future to think about.

Ophelia: Why can't my future include a relationship with Hamlet? He says he loves me, and I love him. We both want to get married to each other, so where's the problem?

Polonius: Don't be naive! I raised you better than to assume everyone is honest and forthright about their feelings, especially with romantic intentions. Just look at your brother. He understands how romance works.

Ophelia (*aside*): Yeah, we'll see how that turns out when his dick falls off.

Polonius: Ophelia, I'll be honest- I was disappointed when you chose to be born a woman, but I've come to love you regardless. And as a man, there are some things I need to teach you about womanhood.

Ophelia: (*flatly*) Please, teach me, father.

Polonius: Well, it's like this: men are disgusting beasts with only one thing on their minds. They will literally say or do anything to get what they want. They'll pretend to have emotions in order to take advantage of you. We've all accepted that this is the way of the world and that nothing could be done to help it. However,

18

I.III

(Polonius cont.)
because you're a woman, we hold you to a higher standard even though everyone knows that your brains are smaller and you are all easily fooled. It's common knowledge that women don't take any pleasure in sex and that it's solely a tool to make more Christian babies. So, you can't be tempted by Hamlet's sweet words because he'll sully your virginal purity and then where will you be when you start searching for a husband? Every man wants to marry a woman with zero sexual experience so that when they consummate their marriage it's an unpleasant and humiliating experience, just as God intended. Why the first night with your mother was so horrible and awkward that I was barely able to achieve climax-

Ophelia: Please get to the point.

Polonius: Yes, well all I am trying to say is that you should stay away from Hamlet if you know what's good for your future.

Ophelia: Duly noted, Dad. I'm going to go…be somewhere else.

Exit Ophelia

I.IV

Scene IV

**Outside the Castle Gates.
Bernardo is standing at his post half-asleep.**

Enter Hamlet, Horatio, and Marcellus.

Hamlet: Hoo boy, it's cold tonight.

Horatio: Yeah, I couldn't imagine coming out and doing this every single night as my job.

Both look at Bernardo, who says nothing but looks annoyed.

Hamlet: What time is it now?

Horatio: Well, since it's been a minute since you last asked, I'm gonna say just after midnight.

Marcellus (*checking his wrist*): Yep, my sundial reads midnight.

Horatio: That's not how sundials…(*shakes head*) In any case, if it's after midnight then that means the ghost should appear any minute. (*Trumpets blow*) Woah, what was that?

Hamlet: Ugh, it's this stupid drinking game the King plays. Every time he chugs his drink, they sound the trumpets.

Horatio: Is this a new game?

Hamlet: Nope. There's a long tradition in this country of getting blackout drunk. To be honest, I think it makes us look like a bunch of idiots to the rest of the world. Everyone just thinks that we're a gaggle of loud, obnoxious morons. But, people kinda write off all the messed up shit they do by saying "oh, I was just drunk," but it's hard to take anyone seriously when you've seen them piss their pants and pass out. People don't forget about that kind of stuff.

(Hamlet cont.)
Like that one time where Horatio pooped on the-

Horatio: Look, it's the ghost!

Enter Ghost, who stands far away from the group.

Marcellus clears his throat and holds out his hand. Hamlet places money in his hand.

Hamlet: I'll be damned! Papa! It's you! Talk to me, please. Tell me why you're here! Why aren't you up in heaven? God's gonna be so pissed when he realizes you're missing. It must be really important for you to come all the way back to this hellhole, especially wearing all that heavy armor. Do you have something you need to tell me? Maybe something about how much you miss your little fancy boy? Tell me what you want!

Ghost beckons to Hamlet

Horatio: It looks like it wants you to follow it.

Marcellus: I wouldn't do that if I were you. One time I followed a ghost and it hit me in the head with a rock and stole my pants.

Horatio: Yeah, Hamlet, it could be a trick.

Hamlet: He's not talking with all of you standing around. Clearly, he's shy and wants to speak to me alone. I'm gonna go.

Horatio: Don't go, Hamlet! It might try to suck your blood or grind your bones to make its bread.

Hamlet: (*after a pause of consideration*) Meh. I had a good run. What harm could it do?

Horatio: Uh…what if it leads you over the edge of a cliff and you

I.IV

(**Horatio cont.**)
die? Or what if it makes you go completely insane and sets off a chain of events that causes you and everyone you care about to die? What if that chain of events leads to the destruction of the entire country?

Hamlet: I said "meh". What more do you want? I'm gonna see what it's all about.

Horatio: Listen, man, I'm telling you I've got a really bad feeling about all this. I mean, you're the prince so you're clearly going to do whatever you want, but I'm just saying that if you go with this ghost I think something terrible is going to happen.

Hamlet: You guys are just a bunch of scardy-cats. I ain't afraid of no ghost. He might know some cool stuff. It'll just be a minute.

Marcellus: Grab him! He's already infected with ghost-madness!

Hamlet: Keep your hands off me! I'm not infected with anything.

Hamlet leaves with Ghost.

Horatio (*shaking his head*): Nothing good will come of this.

Marcellus: We should probably follow him. If I know ghosts, he's probably already on the ground bleeding from his rock-wound.

Horatio: Eh, I don't know. Hamlet said he wanted to speak with the ghost in private.

Marcellus: C'moooooon. Something is clearly going on here.

Horatio: That sounds like not-my-problem.

Marcellus: Well, you do what you want, but I'm gonna go after

(Marcellus cont.)
him.

Exit Marcellus.

Horatio: (*after a beat*) Goddamn it.

Exit Horatio

Bernardo wakes up, looks around, and falls back asleep.

Scene V

Slightly further away from Outside the Castle Gates.

Enter Ghost and Hamlet

Hamlet: Okay, that's far enough. I'm not going any further. (*squints at Ghost*) Hey, you do have a beard!

Ghost: Listen carefully.

Hamlet: Okay.

Ghost: I don't have a lot of time before I go back to burning in agony in purgatory.

Hamlet: Oh. That sucks.

Ghost: Eh, it's not that bad. But there's something you need to do.

Hamlet: Tell me, I'll do anything for you, Papa.

Ghost: Anything? Even... (*Dramatically*) revenge?

Hamlet: What?

Ghost: I'm your father, the King Big Hamlet himself. I am cursed to walk the night and burn in agony in purgatory during the day until the sins of my past are cleansed from my spirit. Oh, the things I could tell you about the afterlife my son. They would make your blood run cold! They would make your eyes rolls back in your head and your hair stand on end! It's truly amazing and wondrous and awe-inspiring! However, it's completely against the Ghost-code to tell you anything about it, so...

Hamlet: Okay…

I.V

Ghost: Anyways, you need to revenge my mysterious and suspicious...(*dramatically*) murder!

Hamlet: Murder?!

Ghost: That's right... (*dramatically*) murder! Murder most foul. Murder under mysterious and suspicious circumstances!

Hamlet: Just tell me who did it, Papa, and I'll revenge the shit out of them.

Ghost: Very good! Now, listen, what I am about to tell you is secret. Which means you can't go blabbing to any of your drunken friends. But this is how everything happened: I was sleeping in the orchard underneath my napping tree when a serpent came out and bit me...

Hamlet: You want me to revenge a snake?

Ghost: Shut up and keep listening! It's not just any snake that got me. This snake is now the new king of Denmark!

Hamlet: I knew it! Uncle Claudius! Wait, he bit yo-

Ghost: Yep, my incestuous, adulterous piece of trash brother is the one behind all this. And to make things worse he completely seduced your mother. It's kind of crazy how she forgot about me, the man she pledged to love forever, so quick, isn't it? I mean, I guess my brother and I look alike, but come on. I'm clearly the more handsome of the two...

Hamlet: (*pretending to clear his throat*) Get to the point.

Ghost: Yes, well, anyways, I was sleeping under my napping tree when your uncle came around with a vial of ear-poison. As you know, ear-poison is the deadliest of all poisons, so I was a goner. And that was that. He took my life, my crown, and my wife. So

I.V

(Ghost cont.)
now it's your job to make sure that your uncle gets his dose of vitamin justice. But don't let things get out of hand. I know you're probably mad at your mother, too, but don't take it out on her. Believe me, she'll get hers in the afterlife. (*Rooster crows and Ghost puts hands over ears*) Ugh, that sound. (*sneezes*) My sinuses… I gotta go. Back to burning in agony in purgatory.

Ghost exits

Hamlet: I think I need to sit down. (*rubs his eyes*) I can do this. I'll forget everything I ever knew that doesn't have to do with getting revenge. This is my new life now. This is my purpose and I will do everything I can in my power to make sure that smirking piece of shit uncle of mine gets what's coming to him. No price is too high to pay. God damn my mother...No, remember what Papa said... Uncle Claudius is the one who must suffer. I swear he will pay.

Horatio (*off stage*): My lord?

Marcellus (*off stage*): Prince Hamlet?

Horatio (*off stage*): I hope we're not too late!

Marcellus (*off stage*): The ghost probably already got him with its rock.

Hamlet: Over here!

Horatio (*off-stage*): Stay right there, my lord!

Hamlet: I'm not going anywhere.

Enter Horatio and Marcellus

Marcellus: Oh, you're up. I guess this was a friendly ghost.

I.V

Horatio: Did it talk to you?

Hamlet: Yes, and it was mostly good news.

Horatio: Well, tell us!

Hamlet: No, I know you idiots can't keep your mouths shut.

Horatio: Hey, you already paid us off. We're sworn to secrecy.

Marcellus: It's true.

Hamlet: You swear?

Horatio: Yes.

Hamlet: You really swear?

Horatio and Marcellus: We swear.

Hamlet: Okay. There's a seriously bad dude living in Denmark.

Horatio: Well, yeah, obviously. We didn't need a ghost to tell us that. There's tons of bad dudes everywhere!

Hamlet: Yes, of course. Welp, that's that. I think we better go our separate ways for a while. I know you guys are busy and I've got a lot of business to attend to right now. Just mountains of paperwork and meetings after meetings. There's no way I'm getting home at 5 pm tonight! Definitely going to be burning the midnight oil on this one...

Horatio: Slow down, there, Hamlet. You're not making any sense.

Hamlet: I'm sorry if I offend you. I'm just very busy is all.

Horatio: I'm not offended, I'm just worried-

I.V

Hamlet: Oh, there's offense. By St. Patrick I can hear the offense in your voice. And...well, listen. The ghost opened up my mind to a lot of stuff. I've got a bunch of work I need to do. I need to ask you guys a favor.

Horatio: What is it?

Hamlet: I need you guys to never tell anyone about what you saw here tonight. Don't mention the ghost to anyone else, either, okay?

Horatio: Sure, fine, whatever.

Marcellus: You already paid me off, so we're fine.

Hamlet (*holds out pinky finger*): No, pinky swear.

Horatio (*looks at Marcellus and shrugs*): Uh, okay.

Horatio and Marcellus link their pinkies with Hamlet.

Horatio and Marcellus: We pinky swear.

Hamlet: Great. Now, swear on my sword, too.

Horatio (*annoyed*): We already pinky swore. Everyone knows that's the most sacred promise a man can make.

Marcellus: It's true.

Hamlet: I would just feel a lot better if you also swore on my sword.

Ghost (*off-stage*): Swear!

Hamlet: See, even the ghost wants you to swear!

I.V

Horatio: Uh...okay, just tell us what to say.

Hamlet: Promise you never tell anyone about this!

Ghost (*off-stage*): Swear!

Hamlet: (*to Ghost*) Hold your horses! I'm trying to get them to swear. (*to Horatio and Marcellus*) Okay, guys, just put your hands on my sword and swear and we'll be all on our way.

Ghost (*off-stage*): Swear!

Hamlet: Jesus! Just give me a minute!

Horatio: This is bizarre.

Hamlet: I know, I know. But there are even stranger things happening that you have no idea about. Just humor me, please. Over the next couple days I'm going to be acting crazy.

Horatio (*aside*): Sounds like he's already started acting crazy.

Hamlet: I may say some weird or hurtful things, but remember I'm only pretending. I'm actually going crazy like a fox. But if anyone asks, just tell them you have no idea what's going on. I need you guys to do this for my secret plan to work. Now swear you will.

Ghost (*off-stage*): Swear!

Hamlet (*annoyed*): Shut up! Anyways, thanks guys. I really appreciate your help. I couldn't do this without you. Just remember: you promised not to tell anyone about any of this. Now let's go. I've got a ton of work to do to set things right. Come on!

Hamlet exits.

Horatio: So, are we not swearing on the sword, then?

ABC
Act II

Crazy...
Like a Fox

Scene I

Polonius and Reynaldo are in a room at Polonius' house.

Polonius: Okay, here's the money and the note, Reynaldo. Make sure Laertes gets it.

Reynaldo: Sure thing.

Polonius: You are going to do a fantastic job, I just know it. But before you go and visit him, make sure to ask around to see what he's been up to.

Reynaldo (*strained*): Yep.

Polonius: Good. Just to be clear, make sure to ask around and see where all of the shifty people in Paris are. Don't be afraid to get your hands dirty to find out who they are and what they do and how they get their money and what they eat for breakfast. Try to find out what kind of company they keep. Then, just kind of casually slip in the question of whether or not they know my son. Don't act like you're his best friend, just pretend you're a casual acquaintance.

Reynaldo: I've only met your son once, so...

Polonius: Seriously though, just say something like "Oh, I don't know him well, but I've heard he's a crazy guy into a lot of crazy stuff." And then make up some crazy stuff to say, but not too crazy. We don't want to besmirch the family name, after all. Just, you know, the usual stuff that boy his age get into.

Reynaldo: Like what?

Polonius: Oh, you know, drinking, gambling, killing people in duels, the usual mischief.

II.I

Reynaldo: Uh....

Polonius: I know, I know. You're worried that you might make my boy look bad. But it's all about presentation. You see, if you mention these things in a lighthearted way nobody will think twice of it.

Reynaldo: Isn't that just going to make his reputation worse?

Polonius: Listen, you're not understanding. All you're doing here is priming the pump. See, you mention some stuff you heard and strike up a conversation with one of these bottom-feeders and get them going by telling them about your past. And then they start talking and telling you about the stuff that they've done. For example, if you were to get me going about the things I've done, I'd probably start telling you about the time Claudius and I entered a brothel with a donkey and a honeycomb and... wait, what was I saying again?

Reynaldo (*aside*): The hell if I know. (*to Polonius*) I believe you were talking about priming the pump.

Polonius: Ah yes. You prime the pump by confessing some things of your own to get them to confess. When they admit to knowing Laertes, they'll start talking about what he's been up to. "Oh, I saw him go to this casino, or that brothel." So, your little lie is the bait on the hook that catches the truth. Sometimes the road to the truth involves walking the winding path of lies. It's a little trick that men of wisdom, like myself, use to find things out and what you will use to find out what my son has been doing. Do you understand?

Reynaldo (*annoyed*): Yes.

Polonius: Okay, great. Well, that's all. Thanks for all your hard work.

Reynaldo: Okay, I'm going to go now.

II.I

Polonius: Don't forget to prime the pump!

Reynaldo (*pretending not to hear*): Sorry, I can't hear you I'm too far away...

Polonius: Good luck!

Exit Reynaldo.

Enter Ophelia.

Polonius: There's my second-favorite child! Why the long face, Ophelia?

Ophelia: Something weird just happened.

Polonius: What happened?

Ophelia: Well, I was sitting in my room doing some sewing when Hamlet just barges in. He looked terrible, like he'd just been mugged or like he'd been sleeping under a bridge or something. His clothes were all dirty and torn and he stank. And he just... looked at me with wide, teary eyes.

Polonius: Was he lovesick?

Ophelia: I don't know, but it really freaked me out.

Polonius: Did he say anything?

Ophelia: He walked over to me and grabbed my wrist really hard. I think it might bruise. And he stood there and put his other hand to his head and just...stared at me. Like he was trying to memorize my face. It felt like an eternity. Then, finally, he sighed and let me go and walked backwards out the room, still just... staring at me. It was bizarre and I'm actually really worried about him. I think something is terribly wrong.

II.I

Polonius: I'll say! We need to talk to the king! Hamlet is lovesick. It happened to me once before. Love will make a man do the craziest things, like live out of a dumpster for three weeks waiting for a beautiful maid to return your message. Tell me, what did you do to Hamlet to cause such a reaction?

Ophelia (*incredulous*): I didn't do anything.

Polonius: Well, clearly this has driven him mad. It's okay, Ophelia, it's not all your fault. I'm partially responsible too. I should have been clearer in my instructions and made sure you, my sweet simple daughter, understood what I meant. Now the young prince is going crazy in his love for you. We need to go to the king and tell him what's happening with his son.

Exit Polonius

Ophelia stands in shock and shakes her head.

Ophelia: My father might just be the stupidest man alive. One day it's going to get him killed.

Still shaking head, Ophelia follows her father off stage.

Scene II

**King's Throne Room.
King, Queen, Rosencrantz, Guildenstern, other attendants are all standing around.**

King: Welcome Rosenkraut and Guildedstorm! It's great that you could come here on such short notice. We need your help. Hamlet has been acting really weird since his father's mysterious death. At first, we thought it was just gloominess, but it's clear that it's something much more. Since you two are such good friends with Hamlet, we were hoping you'd do us a major favor and talk to him for us.

Queen: It would really mean the world to us. Hamlet has always spoken about how much he loves the two of you. He trusts you two, so it shouldn't be hard to get him to tell you what's bothering him. Plus, if you do help us, we'll be sure to make it worth your while.

Rosencrantz: I mean, it's not so much a favor as an order…

Guildenstern: …so we don't have much choice, do we?

King: That's right!

Queen: Thank you for your service, Rossenkoot and Googlystern! Go and see Hamlet straight away. One of the servants will take you.

Guildenstern: Always happy to betray a friend's trust, my queen.

Queen: And we are so grateful for that.

Exit Rosencrantz and Guildenstern and attendant.

II.II

Enter Polonius

Polonius: The ambassadors have returned from Norway, your grace!

King: This better be good news.

Polonius: Oh, it is, my lord. Plus, I did a little detective work and I think I've found the cause of Hamlet's craziness! Some would say that ol' Polonius has been losing his marbles in his old age and while that may be true, let it stand here and now that I am probably the world's greatest detective, well, perhaps not the greatest since there are some good-

King: Please, tell us what you've found.

Polonius: No, let's hear the ambassadors first! I want to save the best news for last!

King: Sure, fine, whatever. Bring'em in.

Exit Polonius

King: You hear that, Gertrude? He says he found out what's wrong with Hamlet. We didn't need to pay those two idiots after all…

Queen: I'll bet it's his father's death and our quick marriage. Hamlet was never a fan of weddings.

King: We'll see.

Enter Polonius with Ambassadors

King: So, what's the word in Norway? Are they gonna stop with the Radical Norwegian Terrorism or what?

Ambassador: So, we went and spoke with the King of Norway

(**Ambassador cont.**)
himself in Norway. Have you ever been? Beautiful this time of year. Anyways, this whole thing is a misunderstanding. He's not mad at us. All that war stuff and taking lands from Norway is totally in the past. He's over it. These days, he's going against the Polish for…reasons. So, he told young Fortinbras to cut it out with the Radical Norwegian Terrorism and gave him a bit of hush money. But he does need a favor from us. (*produces a paper*) He requests passage through Denmark so that he can march his army against the Polish.

King: This is hyuge. Simply tremendous news. I told you I was the only one who could end this Radical Norwegian Terrorism. This is a proud day for Denmark! I never liked those dirty Polacks anyways. We will give the Norwegians passage to march against them. Good job, guys. Clearly you flourished under my expert leadership. Now get out.

Exit Ambassadors

Polonius: Ah, my king and queen, you two are the embodiment of grace, justice, and duty. Why, day wouldn't be day and night wouldn't be night, time wouldn't even be time without your royal presence. And since brevity is the soul of wit, and I am among the wittiest and therefore brevity-est in the entire Kingdom, I shall keep this message short. And this message is, Hamlet is crazy. Crazy! Off his rocker! Out to lunch! Bonkers! Coocoo for Coacoa Puffs! Out of his mind!

Queen: Please, get to the point.

Polonius: I'm getting there! Just let me set the scene. He's nuts. It's true. It's a real shame. It's a real shame that it's true. And true that it's a real shame. At any rate: Hamlet is crazy. And we've been trying to figure out why. And I submit to you: I have a daughter. And she's a sweet and simple girl who, like every proper woman, does exactly what a man orders her to. And I ordered her to tell me if

II.II

(Polonius cont.)
there was anything going on with Hamlet. When she refused, I put my detective skills to the test and found this letter from Hamlet! (*Produces letter and reads from it.*) "Roses are red, your name's not Amelia. Do you wanna make out with me? My dear sweet Ophelia."

Queen: Hamlet wrote that? I had no idea he was such a talented poet!

Polonius: Yes! He wrote hundreds of lines of poetry as beautiful and eloquent as these you see here!

King: So, did she make out with him or what?

Polonius: What do I look like to you, my dear king?

King: Do you really want me to answer that?

Polonius: No, because I know what you are going to say! I am a man of faith and honor. When my daughter told me about how Hamlet wanted to be with her, I sat her down and I said "Listen, Ophelia, I love you like a daughter, but Hamlet is a prince and you're honestly not that great a catch. So, you need to refuse his advances because it's never going to happen between the two of you." And then I took it upon myself to refuse every gift and message Hamlet sent to her. And Hamlet, heartbroken and sad, began fasting which caused his brains turned to mush from lack of protein and caused him to go completely crazy. And that solves the mystery of how the Prince lost his mind!

King: Hmm…what do you think, Gertrude?

Queen: Yeah, sure, that sounds right.

Polonius: Have I ever been wrong before?

II.II

King: Well, now that you mention it, those pills you sold haven't made my hands any bigger-

Polonius: I told you that results will vary! At any rate, if I'm wrong about the prince, you can take this (*points at head*) away from this (*points at neck*). But we need to know for sure.

King: And how do you plan on finding out for sure?

Polonius: I've heard that the prince likes to stand around smoking clove cigarettes in the throne room, sometimes for hours at a time.

Queen: Yes, he calls that his "glower hours."

Polonius: Okay, so here's what we can do. When Hamlet is having his glower hours, I'll send Ophelia out to talk to him and we'll hide behind the curtain and listen in. If he doesn't start begging her to talk to him, I'll resign my post and become a turnip farmer.

King: You had me at "resign my post".

Queen: Here comes Hamlet now with a book! I didn't even know he could read.

Polonius: Okay, get out of here and I'll test the waters. Go on, get!

Exit King, Queen, and Attendants.

Enter Hamlet reading a book

Polonius (*acting too casual*): Oh, hello Hamlet. Didn't see you there. How are you?

Hamlet: Uh…

Polonius: Do you remember me, my lord?

II.II

Hamlet: Of course, I do! You're the village idiot, right?

Polonius: Uh…no.

Hamlet: Oh, I guess I had you mixed up with someone else.

Polonius: I suppose you did.

Hamlet: The sun breeding maggots in a dead dog is really just God blessing the corpse with new life. You have a daughter, correct?

Polonius: Uh…yes.

Hamlet: Then keep her out of the sun. God gifts us all with new life through the sun, but you wouldn't want her to get that gift. It's happened before you know.

Polonius (*aside*): I knew it! He's talking about Ophelia! I think he wants to get her pregnant. At first, he thought I was the village idiot, and only a madman would confuse an intellectual giant like myself with the village idiot.

Hamlet: You know I can hear you right now.

Polonius (*aside, ignoring/talking over Hamlet*): Oh, this is much worse than I thought, and I've gone through some pretty bad spells of lovesickness myself when I was his age. Lemme try to get more info out of him. *(to Hamlet)* What're you reading there, my lord?

Hamlet: Words, mostly.

Polonius: On what matter?

Hamlet: Paper?

Polonius: I mean, what are you reading about?

II.II

Hamlet: Ah, it's just a story about how men get old and grow gray beards and have wrinkled faces and weak hams. I mean, it's all true, but I can't help doubting it. You're old like the men in my book, Polonius, but wouldn't you become young like me if you could walk backwards like a crab?

Polonius (*aside*): He's crazy, my hams are as strong as ever! (to Hamlet) So are you gonna step out of the air then?

Hamlet: To where? Into my grave?

Polonius: Well, that's out of the air, yes. (*aside*) For such a crazy and lovesick fool, he's still has some wits about him. I don't know if I can reach him..

Hamlet: I can still hear you…

Polonius: (*ignoring and talking over Hamlet*): I'll leave him now and find a way to get him to meet with Ophelia. (*to Hamlet*) My lord, I must take my leave to go…uh…return some video tapes.

Hamlet: You can't take anything from me that I would willingly give to you, except my life, I guess. But who would want that?

Polonius: Okay, well on that note, goodbye!

Hamlet: What a fucking moron.

Enter Rosencrantz and Guildenstern

Polonius: Hamlet is over there. Go see how he's doing.

Exit Polonius

Guildenstern: Dude!

Rosencrantz: Dude!

II.II

Hamlet: Dude! Rosencrantz, Guildenstern! What's up guys?!

Rosencrantz: Eh, nothing.

Guildenstern: Can't complain, you know. Just not on top of Lady Luck.

Hamlet: But not getting crushed under her foot, right?

Rosencrantz: I guess not, no.

Hamlet: So, you're somewhere around her waist then?

Guildenstern: Hopefully a little lower.

Hamlet: (*laughs*) Yeah, we all wish for that. What's up?

Rosencrantz: Eh, nothing much. Finally lost my virginity, so that's cool.

Hamlet: Then the end of the world must be coming soon! What brings you guys to this dumpster?

Guildenstern: What dumpster?

Hamlet: I mean Denmark. This place sucks. I can't wait to get out of here after I graduate.

Rosencrantz: If this is a dumpster, I'm afraid to hear what you think of the rest of the world.

Hamlet: The whole world is a giant trash heap alright, but Denmark is easily the biggest stinkiest pile of doo-doo in the whole world.

Rosencrantz: Come on, it's not that bad.

II.II

Hamlet: That's your opinion. Maybe it all depends on your attitude. And my attitude is that Denmark sucks.

Rosencrantz: Why don't you just change your attitude then?

Hamlet (*sarcastically*): Wow, I hadn't thought of that! I'll just go ahead and change my outlook! Thanks guys! Life is so much better now.

Guildenstern: All right, Jesus, take it easy. He was just saying it might be a good idea to change your perspective a little.

Hamlet: What is perspective anyways?

Guildenstern: I don't know. But one thing I do know is that perspective is constantly changing so there's no point in getting hung up on any one moment.

Hamlet: Yeah, I guess. I dunno. Let's go and grab a drink. All this talk is giving me a headache.

Rosencrantz and Guildenstern: We'll buy the first round, my lord.

Hamlet: Aw, come on guys. You aren't my servants. You're my bros. And even though I really am happy to see you, I still don't know what you're doing here.

Rosencrantz: To visit with you and definitely not for any other reason.

Hamlet: That's great…you sure there was no other reason for you to come? You can tell me. It's not a big deal if there's some other business you need to attend to.

Guildenstern: What do you want us to say?

Hamlet: Anything, as long as it's the truth. I have a feeling you

II.II

were summoned. You seem like you're hiding something. I mean, I know you guys pretty well and, no offense, you both are way too dumb to lie to me. I know the King and Queen sent for you.

Rosencrantz: (*nervous*) Now…why would they do something like that?

Hamlet: You tell me. Before you speak, just remember, we go way back. You guys have been my ride or die homies since we were little. All I'm asking for is the truth. I don't think that's too much to ask for as your bro.

Rosencrantz (*aside to Guildenstern*): Dude, what do we do?

Hamlet (*aside to himself*): Let's see what these rats are gonna do.

Guildenstern: All right, you got us. We were summoned.

Hamlet: Before you start trying to guess why you guys were asked to keep an eye on me, I'll just tell you. I've been pretty depressed lately. Everything I used to love doesn't bring me any happiness anymore. The whole world just seems…shitty. Even this amazing castle that I live in is just another piece of garbage. I don't know what's wrong with me. Everything is just terrible. And I can't help but feel like humanity is just a big joke. We walk around talking about how noble and smart we are, but the truth is we're just animals. We talk about God and morality and the beauty of the world and what do we do? We destroy his creation and elevate the most selfish and wicked among us to the highest positions of power. We're just a bunch of stupid monkeys screeching into the night. Nothing brings me any kind of happiness anymore: men don't make me happy, women don't make me happy... What's so funny?

Rosencrantz: Nothing.

Hamlet: Then why were you grinning when I said that people don't make me happy?

II.II

Rosencrantz: Well, I guess I was smiling because you said men don't make you happy and we met some performers on the way over here. We thought a surprise show would cheer you up, but I guess not.

Hamlet: What do they perform? Eh, I'm sure the King will enjoy their acting whatever it is. I'll have to sit and watch, but it won't do anything for me.

Guildenstern: They might be right up your alley since they perform tragedies.

Hamlet: Wow, what are the odds they were coming here? Shouldn't they be making tons of money in the city?

Guildenstern: I think things have changed. Maybe they found out you were gloomy and wanted to cheer you up.

Hamlet: I don't know about that. My gloominess is a well-kept secret. Are they still pulling in big crowds?

Rosencrantz: I don't think so.

Hamlet: Well, why are they coming here? Are they getting rusty and need practice?

Rosencrantz: No, they're still good. I think they got into a gang-war with a bunch of child actors muscling in on their turf. The common folk love watching the kids blurt out their lines, but all the upper class people are terrified to show their faces at the kid's performances because they're afraid they're going to be written into one of their next plays to look like a buncha idiots.

Hamlet: Child actors? Who's watching them? How do they travel? Are they getting paid, or is it just for exposure? What happens when they grow up? Does the fame get to their heads and they become drug addicts and spiral out of control because being famous

45

II.II

(Hamlet cont.)
as a small child fucks you up psychologically?

Rosencrantz: Yeah, it's a big mess. All we know for sure is that the adult actors and the child actors are in a blood-feud and I guess things went south real quick because the adult actors took their show on the road. I think the child actors have connections to the mob or something.

Hamlet: Really?

Guildenstern: Nobody knows for sure, but that's what the rumors are.

Hamlet: Eh, I guess it's not that crazy. I mean, at one point my piece of shit uncle was a loud-mouthed outsider that was completely ridiculed and now the same people that were talking shit about him are going on and on about how he's such a smart, strong leader. Definitely something for the philosophers to think about.

Sound of Trumpets

Guildenstern: That must be the actors.

Hamlet: Well, anyways, I'm happy to see my bros. So, let me officially welcome you to my home. Now I have to go pretend to be happy to see these actors. They aren't the only ones being deceived either- my uncle-dad and aunt-mom are also being tricked…

Guildenstern: Tricked how?

Hamlet: Oh, they think I've completely lost my mind! But I just want them to think that for…reasons.

Enter Polonius

Polonius: Hello, boys!

II.II

Hamlet (*to Guildenstern and Rosencrantz*): You see that old dude over there? He's still in diapers.

Rosencrantz: Oh yeah, I've heard it's cause old people have weak hams.

Hamlet: Watch, he's going to tell us about the actors and I'm gonna make him think I'm completely bat shit insane. (*to Polonius*) Yes, it did happen on a Monday!

Polonius: I have news, my lord!

Hamlet: Borrrr-ing.

Polonius: There's a group of actors coming!

Hamlet: And a jackass announcing their presence!

Polonius: And they're the best actors in the world! Whether it's comedy, tragedy, history, pastoral, dramedy, pastoral-comedy, sci-fi, dystopian, romance, bondage, dramedy-history, Twilight, sword and sorcery, dramedy-sci-fi-dystopian, or musical sword and sorcery! They've got all the major genres covered.

Hamlet: The king of Israel had a precious treasure.

Polonius: And what treasure was that?

Hamlet: Well…(singing) One fair daughter and no more, who he loved with all his heart!

Polonius (*aside*): Still talking about my daughter.

Hamlet: Ain't it right, you old king of Israel?

Polonius: Well, I do have a daughter, but I don't really love her

II.II

(Polonius cont.)
with all my heart…

Hamlet: That's not how the song goes!

Polonius: Well, what's the next part then?

Hamlet: Eh, I don't remember. What were we talking about again?

Enter Players

Hamlet: Welcome to all of you! Glad to meet you, good to see you! Oh, Haven't seen you in a while. What's good, homie? Oh, looking beautiful miss, looking more beautiful since the last time I saw you! Fantastic to see all of you! Please, give us all a little taste of your talent now!

First Player: Uh, okay, what should we do?

Hamlet: Uh, I think I heard you guys give this speech once. I don't know if it was even an official performance. I remember that nobody even really liked it all that much. But I did, along with a few other members of the audience with more...refined tastes. A lot of people were complaining that the lines were too...ordinary. That they didn't have art or feeling or beauty in the words. But I thought it was beautiful because of its simplicity and honesty. Things don't always need to be dressed up and fancy. Sometimes simple language is the best way to get the point across.

Polonius: I disagree! How will people know how smart you are if you don't use tremendous words egregiously to showcase a superlative and refined intellectual capacity?

First Player: I mean, that's all well and good, but I don't know what speech you're talking about. Are you sure it was us?

Hamlet: It was a beautiful speech. The language was so rich and

(Hamlet cont.)
real. As if a regular person were speaking the lines instead of all these crazy "thithers" and "thous". I think you were even swearing, which I would say adds even more to the authenticity. It was a damn good speech.

Polonius: Profanity! In live-action theatre?! I cannot think of a more despicable, mortifying, and scandalous blasphemy! The theatre is the highest form of art there is. It is a place for poetry and beauty and not low-class language that you are advocating.

First Player: Seriously though, I don't think we were the one that performed this...

Hamlet: Well, all right, in any case, it was great and I liked it and I'd love to see you guys do something similar. (*to Polonius*) All right, can you take these actors to their rooms? If you don't, I have a feeling they're gonna be talking a whole lot of shit about you.

Polonius: Okay. (*aside to Hamlet*) I'll set them up in our most modest rooms. You know how things grow feet around actors.

Hamlet: No, I don't think you heard me correctly. Take them to a nice room. We want our guests to feel welcome. Take them to your room if you can't find ones nice enough for them.

Polonius: Uh, I think we'll find somewhere else. Come along, everyone.

Hamlet: Polonius will take you to where you need to go! (*to First Player*) Hang on a second, friend. Can you guys perform the Murder of Gonzago?

First Player: Yeah.

Hamlet: Awesome. Perform it tomorrow night. I also want you to add a scene from my fan fiction to it.

II.II

First Player: Uh....

Hamlet: Don't worry, it's nothing dirty. I just think it'll make the story more...relevant to our audience. I'll get the lines to you later. Now get outta here you scamp!

Exit First Player

Hamlet: All right, guys, you two remember where your old rooms are. Go ahead and catch some z's. Mi casa es su casa.

Rosencrantz: I don't know what that means, but I like the way you said it.

Hamlet: All right, now get on out of here! I've got brooding to do.

Exit Rosencrantz and Guildenstern

Hamlet: Alone at last. I really hope this works out. I know it's a long shot, but maybe this will get him to confess. I don't know. I have to do something. Am I just going to sit here like a coward while the guy who murdered my father is busy banging my mother? I gotta take my revenge. But, I gotta know for sure. Hopefully, my uncle is dumb enough to admit his own guilt. I'll have the actors put on a performance that'll be very similar to what the ghost told me happened. If my uncle seems guilty, that's when I'll make my move.

II.II

Act III

Want to Read My Fan Fiction?

Scene I

**King's Throne Room.
King, Queen, Polonius, Ophelia, Rosencrantz, and Guildenstern are holding court.**

King: So, anyways, after they disposed of the body, everyone carried on with the party like nothing happened. Though there was some blood on the beautiful marble floor, which was a real shame… Oh, that reminds me, Rossencoot, Giddystooge, have you figured out why the prince has been acting so crazy?

Rosencrantz: Well, he said himself that he's been feeling a little off but won't say what's been bothering him.

Guildenstern: Yeah, he says he's going crazy like a fox. I think he's just regular crazy though…

Queen: Well, was he happy to see you?

Rosencrantz: Yeah, he seemed happy.

Guildenstern: Happy enough anyways. I think there was something bothering him, some gloominess he was trying to hide from us.

Rosencrantz: He didn't really have anything interesting to say.

Queen: Did you try getting him drunk?

Guildenstern: We were going to, but a bunch of actors came around out of nowhere and he started rambling about his fan fiction. The actors are all hanging around drinking all our wine and making out in the hallways. At least Hamlet seems excited about their show.

Polonius: Yes, it's true. He begged me to request your royal presence at the show.

III.I

King: That's hyuge news! I'm glad the prince is happy. Tremendous job, Rudycrat and Gogglestup. The next time you see him confirm we'll be at the show! This might just be our miracle cure. Now go on and get outta here.

Rosencrantz: Uh, okay, sure. Thanks.

Exit Rosencrantz and Guildenstern

King: Gertrude, my sweet, you need to leave, too. Hamlet is coming and we've arranged for him to "run into" Ophelia. Polonius and I are going to spy on him and see if it really is his love for Ophelia that's causing him to act so crazy. If you hang around, we're just gonna get distracted trying to sneak a peek down your dress.

Queen: Of course, my king. (*to Ophelia*) Ophelia, even though you're only a five at best, I really hope that you're the reason that Hamlet is going crazy. You know, you could easily be a six if you just put on some mascara…

Ophelia (*rolling her eyes*): Duly noted.

Queen: Okay, well, good luck!

Exit Queen

Polonius: Okay, Ophelia, stand here. I wish we had a push-up bra for you now. The Queen is right, mascara really would knock you up a few points. Oh well. Okay, pretend to read this book, even though you don't know how to read-

Ophelia: I read all the time.

Polonius (*ignoring*): because everyone knows when a woman reads a book, it's solely because she's lonely and wants a man to talk to her. Okay, great, looking…okay. Trap is set. You know, it's inter

(Polonius cont.)
esting how you can gloss over any kind of wrongdoing with a pretty face.

King (*aside*): Polonius is right. I wonder how much I've gotten away with because of how gorgeous I am.

Polonius: Your grace, I hear the prince coming! Let's hide!

King and Polonius attempt to hide by standing behind a single newspaper.

Enter Hamlet

Hamlet: To be or not to be, that's the question. On the one hand, there's beauty in the struggle for survival, in the fight against pain and misfortune. But on the other, isn't it best to end your life on your own terms? In death, there's no more pain, no more heartache or any of the other day to day bullshit we need to put up with in our sad little human existence. It's something to wish for. To sleep and dream forever. And there's the rub- we don't know what kind of dreams we have when we leave this mortal coil. And that's what keeps us here. Who would put up with all of this pain and craziness if we knew there was something better on the other side? Who would deal with broken hearts or the tangles of law or shithead politicians or the back-breaking, mind-numbing toil of work? The only thing keeping us here is the fear of something worse on the other side. Death makes cowards of us all and so we don't do anything and live our lives constantly looking over our shoulders waiting for that inevitable moment where we leave this world forever...

Ophelia: Talking to yourself again?

Hamlet: Oh, uh, hey, Ophelia. I didn't see you there.

Ophelia looks at her father, who gestures for her to make her move.

III.I

Ophelia (*disaffected*): (*sighs*) Hey, uh, I have some of the gifts you gave me. I think you should take them back. (*aside to Hamlet*) My idiot father is forcing me to give it all back to you. He's watching right now.

Hamlet (*examining the stuff*): I don't think I gave you any of this.

Ophelia: (*concerned*) Uh, you did. See? This is that poem you wrote me. The perfume you gave me for my birthday. The card you gave me for Valentine's day. Look, it's got your signature right here.

Hamlet: Nope, wasn't me. Probably some other Hamlet.

Ophelia: Is something wrong? You've been acting really strange lately and well, I'm getting worried about you. (*takes his hand*) You can talk to me, you know.

Hamlet (*pulls hand away*): Let me ask you a question: Are you honest?

Ophelia: Uh, what?

Hamlet: Are you beautiful?

Ophelia: What are you talking about?

Hamlet: I'm just saying, it's probably hard to be both.

Ophelia: …Are you saying that it's only possible to be honest or beautiful?

Hamlet: That's exactly what I'm saying. The power of your beauty will eventually eat away at your honesty until you're just another lying whore. Just look at my mother. She used to be a good woman, but her beauty wore down her honesty until she finally let that serpent into her bed. It'll happen to you one day, too, which is why

III.I

(**Hamlet cont.**)
I don't love you anymore.

Ophelia (*hurt*): You don't? …You don't mean that.

Hamlet (*flat, disaffected*): I do. It's nothing personal. It's just…I'd rather spare myself the pain of watching you become corrupted.

Ophelia (*choking back tears*): Stop saying that. What makes you think I would do that? Why do you think I would ever do anything to hurt you?

Hamlet: You really want to keep from hurting me? Go become a nun. That way, you won't have any kids and bring any more shitty people into the world. If my mom never had me, I wouldn't be the prick you see standing before you. I try to be a good person, but everyone thinks I'm losing my mind. Do you realize the choice I have to make right now? How do I even know if I'm making the right call? No…you wouldn't understand. So just… go run off to the nunnery.

Ophelia (*crying*): Hamlet, I can't help you if you won't tell me. Please, just let me know what is going on. I want to help you! I want to help you!

Hamlet: If you don't become a nun, at least do the world a favor and don't have any kids. We have enough shitty people as it is. Now go on and leave me alone.

Ophelia (*crying and reaching out to him*): Hamlet, you aren't well. You're not thinking clearly. But I can help you. Whatever it is that's bothering you, I can help you. Just let me in, just let me help you. Please.

Hamlet shoves her to the floor as he starts to storm out.

Hamlet: You women are all the same. You hide behind your beauty

III.I

(Hamlet cont.)
and your painted cheeks and sweet words, but what's underneath? Lies. Pain. Corruption. You think you're all so innocent the way you dance and sing and come up with cute little nicknames for things, but I know the truth. My mother has shown me what all women are destined to become, that marriage is just a game to them, that there is no such thing as love. Leave me alone.

Exit Hamlet

Ophelia (*still crumpled on the floor*): Hamlet, wait! (*Wipes eyes*) He's so much worse than before. Something horrible is happening. Oh, my poor Hamlet, my poor sweet prince. He's lost his mind completely and now…now I have nobody. Nobody cares…nobody even knows me. What…what am I going to do? (*Buries face in hands and cries*)

King and Polonius emerge from hiding.

King: Well, it's safe to say that your daughter isn't the one causing the problem, Polonius. Honestly, I don't even know if Hamlet is going crazy. I think there's something else going on here. The prince is up to something…I think it might be better if we send him away to some shithole country to clear his head.

Polonius: I think that's a fine plan, my king. However, I still don't think we should rule out the Ophelia theory for the young prince's madness. Ophelia, that was great! Fantastic job. You don't need to tell us what happened, we saw it all. Your grace, before you take any action, I think it would be wise to have his mother speak with him. It seems that he is angry at her for some reason and we might have more progress with her. If she isn't able to get him to talk about what's wrong, then you can ship him off to wherever you'd like to send him.

King: Yes, that sounds like a fine plan. Insanity in powerful individuals must be closely watched.

III.I

King and Polonius leave, Ophelia remains sobbing.

Scene II

A room in the castle. Just as gaudy and overdecorated as the throne room.
Hamlet and the Actors are rehearsing.

Hamlet: Okay, so when you recite the speech from my fan-fic, don't overdo it. I've seen what you actors do when you're not sure how to perform brilliantly-penned writing. You guys always confuse big voices with big emotion and end up screaming at the audience. Or, even worse, you guys don't know what you do with your hands and end up waving them around. We're trying to create an atmosphere here and it would break my heart to see my beautiful writing butchered by some hack trying to steal a scene.

Actor (*loudly, overdramatically, with a flourish of their arms*): Yes! I completely understand.

Hamlet: Good. Don't undersell it either though. Just…use your best judgment. You're a professional after all. I would really hate to see you mumble out my beautiful words when the world needs to hear what I've written! Think of my words as a beautiful woman. Dance with her. Show her a good time. Don't manhandle her though. But don't be a bore, either. Show her something about herself that she never knew. Teach her something she's never heard of, like geography or how to French kiss. You get the idea. Just don't ruin my words. I can't stress the importance of this scene.

Actor (*normal voice*): Yeah, I get it.

Hamlet: Great. Okay, I know you've got a lot of questions about why I'm so hung up on this monologue and the fact is…it's none of your goddamn business. I won't be taking any questions! Go and get ready now. Five minutes to curtain!

All Actors: Thank you, five.

III.II

Exit Actors

Enter Polonius, Rosencrantz, and Guildenstern

Guildenstern: Hey, what's up, dude? Getting ready to show the king your fan-fiction?

Polonius: And the queen, too!

Hamlet: Yes! Go tell the actors to hurry up, please, Polonius!

Exit Polonius

Hamlet: Can you guys go help him? Polonius is easily the dumbest guy I know and will probably screw everything up without you keeping an eye on him.

Rosencrantz: Sure, whatever.

Exit Rosencrantz and Guildenstern

Enter Horatio

Hamlet: Hey, everybody! It's Horatio! Give him a hand! (*Motions for applause*)

Horatio: Uh, who are you talking to?

Hamlet: Why, the audience, of course! (*gestures toward crowd*)

Horatio: Uh….okay…

Hamlet: Ah, I'm just excited to see you, Horatio. You're a good guy. Don't think I'm trying to butter you up, either. I mean, really, what could I even hope to take from you? You don't have anything worth stealing. Nah, you're just a good dude. Look at that face! I could just eat you up! You're a tough little cookie Horatio, taking

III.II

(Hamlet cont.)
everything that comes your way in stride. Let's look at the facts: you're poor, you're stupid, you're ugly,

Horatio: Hey-

Hamlet: -but in many ways because you suffer so much, you don't suffer at all. That's just life for you. Not like me. I've got this... gloominess inside me. But I think things are looking up. They're performing a play tonight and I've convinced them to perform a part of my fan-fiction. No, it's not like that! Nothing dirty. One scene just...resembles how my papa died and I'm gonna see if it produces a reaction. I need you to do me a favor and watch the King throughout the play to see if he looks like he's guilty of murder. If he doesn't, the ghost was a liar and was just sent to trick me after all. Will you help me?

Horatio (*resigned*): Sure thing, Hamlet. I'll keep an eye on him.

Hamlet: I think I hear them coming! I saved you a seat with a good view!

Trumpets blow.

Enter King, Queen, Polonius, Rosencrantz, Guildenstern, Ophelia, and guards

King: There's my nephew-slash-son. How's it going?

Hamlet: Terrific! I've been straight killing it on the market. My stock is up twenty points since this morning. We're gonna run it up the flagpole and shake a few branches to see what comes falling down.

King: Uh...okay. I don't know what to say, son.

Hamlet: Me neither. (*to Polonius*) You used to be an actor, right?

III.II

Polonius: I did! I wasn't bad either. Oh, those were fond days... there's nothing like the theater. Especially the actresses. Why, they were some of the most flexible-

Hamlet: What did you act in?

Polonius: I played Julius Caesar and was struck down at the Capitol by treacherous Brutus!

Hamlet: He must've been a real brute to cap you at the Capitol. Are the actors ready?

Rosencrantz: Yeah. They're waiting for you to start things up.

Queen: Come sit with Mommy, Gus...uh, Hamlet.

Hamlet: Nah, I want to sit over here. (*Hamlet sits by Ophelia*)

Polonius (*aside to King*): See! The Prince is still in love with my daughter!

Hamlet (*to Ophelia*): Do you think I can lie in your lap?

Ophelia (*distant*): I don't think so.

Hamlet: I mean, do you think I can put my head in your lap?

Ophelia: Do what you want.

Hamlet: Did you think I was being dirty there?

Ophelia: It doesn't matter.

Hamlet: There's nothing dirty about lying between a lady's legs.

Ophelia (*distracted*): What?

63

III.II

Hamlet: Nothing, never mind.

Ophelia: You seem to be in a better mood.

Hamlet: Who, me?

Ophelia: Yes.

Hamlet: Well, I can't help but be cheerful on such a glorious day. Look at how happy my mother is and my father only died two hours ago!

Ophelia: Uh…you mean 2 months ago?

Hamlet: Has it been 2 months already? Well, then I guess it's time for me to change out of these black clothes! What am I doing mourning my father when it's been so long? Two months…well, it's comforting to know that a great man's memory will last at least eight weeks. But he needs to be truly great, or everyone will just move on and forget about him.

Trumpets blow

Prologue enters

Hamlet: Ooh, the play's starting. I'm so excited!

Prologue: Tonight we have a story you might already know
A tale of sadness; a tale of woe
Okay, shut up now, we're starting the show.

Exit Prologue

Hamlet: Was that a Prologue or a nursery rhyme?

Ophelia: It was pretty short.

III.II

Hamlet: Just like a woman's love…

Enter Actor King and Actor Queen

Actor King: We've been married for 30 years! Isn't monogamy great?

Actor Queen: Yep! 3 decades of having sex with you and only you and definitely nobody else. Except now it seems like your heart's not in it these days. I'm worried about you. I think you're working too hard.

Actor King: Yeah, probably. Kingin' ain't easy. I'll probably end up working myself to death. But you're tough and beautiful. You'll find yourself a new husband in a second!

Actor Queen: Never! The only way I could ever see myself taking a second husband is by marrying the man who murders you.

Hamlet (*aside*): Interesting.

Actor Queen: But still, a second marriage is a disgrace! I'd basically be killing you all over again every time I'd kiss my second husband.

Actor King: Hmm. Yes, I see what you're saying. But it's easy for you to say that when you're getting d on the reg. When I'm gone, I'll bet you'll change your mind. The thirst is real and there are plenty of other fish in the sea. I'd probably be okay with you moving on to someone else after an appropriate amount of mourning.

Actor Queen: Never! I would never ever move on from you! I'd rather starve to death or die of thirst or do hot yoga! I'd rather spend the rest of my life in jail! I would never ever never remarry!

Hamlet (*aside*): Pssh. Okay.

III.II

Actor King: That's quite the promise. Welp, all this talk of eternal love and monogamy is making me sleepy. I think I'm gonna lay down under my favorite tree, ear up. (*Goes to sleep*)

Actor Queen: Sleep well, my king.

Exit Actor Queen

Hamlet: Mom, what do you think of the play so far?

Queen: I think the lady protests too much.

Hamlet: You don't think she'll keep her word?

King: This argument is ridiculous. There's nothing wrong with multiple marriages. The writers of this play are clearly bought and sold by big monogamy. Sad!

Hamlet: Relax, it's just a joke. You can't be so sensitive that you can't handle a little bit of joking, can you? I thought you were a big strong ruler.

King: I am! There has never been a king as big and strong as I am! What's this play called?

Hamlet: It's called The Mousetrap. It's about a murder in Italy and this king Gonzago and his wife Baptista. I mean, it's just a story and we're all just having a good time, so unless you've got any big secrets weighing on your conscience, I don't see why we can't all just enjoy the show.

Enter Actor dressed as Lucianus

Hamlet: And here comes Lucianus. He's the king's nephew.

Ophelia: Are you going to talk through this whole thing?

III.II

Hamlet: Hey, at least this play is easy to understand. Not like a woman's fickle heart.

Ophelia: Good one.

Hamlet: SHHHHH. Here comes the best part. (*aside*) The part I wrote!

Lucianus: Okay, here we go with the deadly ear poison. Just gonna pour a lil bit right in there… (*pours poison in Actor King's ear*) annnnnnd he's dead and now I'm the new king!

Hamlet: Yeah, so in this part of the completely fictional and not at all real story, the treasonous Lucianus kills the king and takes the throne and gets to bang the Queen, even though they're technically related.

Ophelia: The king, uh, I mean, the real king, is standing up.

Hamlet: (*trying to contain excitement*) Oh, he must be engrossed in the play!

Queen: Is there something wrong, my king?

Polonius: It is just a play, your grace. That man is not dead and has not experienced any harm.

King: This show is over! Turn on the lights! Everyone get the hell out of here, now!

Exit King angrily.

Exit all but Hamlet and Horatio

Hamlet: Well, well, well. Well, well, welly, well-

Horatio: That was something else.

III.II

Hamlet: Come on man, why do you gotta step on my lines? I was getting there. But yeah, looks like the ghost was right after all. You saw his face, right?

Horatio: Yep.

Hamlet: When the poison was mentioned?

Horatio: Mmm-hmm.

Hamlet: Hah! This calls for a celebration! Let's go get drunk!

Enter Rosencrantz and Guildenstern

Guildenstern: Hey, Hamlet, do you have a second?

Hamlet: For you guys? I've got a whole minute.

Guildenstern: Well, it's about the king.

Hamlet: I've heard of him.

Guildenstern: Well, he's pretty upset.

Hamlet: Is he drunk and crying about Bambi's mom again?

Guildenstern: Mmmm…no. He's pretty angry.

Hamlet: What do you want me to do about it? I'm not a doctor or anything. I'll probably just end up getting him more angry.

Guildenstern: Your mom is pretty upset, too. She asked us to come talk to you. Can you tell me what's going on?

Hamlet (*taking an excessively long amount of time*): Um-mmmmmmmmm….no.

III.II

Guildenstern: What?

Hamlet (*shrugging*): No. I can't tell you what's going on here.

Rosencrantz: Okay, well, your mom is freaking out.

Hamlet: Hah. Really? That's awesome.

Rosencrantz: Uh, yeah, I guess? She wants you to come see her in her room before you go to bed.

Hamlet: Well, I should go see her then. Better grab my sword in case I see any snakes along the way. You have any other business for me?

Rosencrantz: Yo, are we…cool, dude?

Hamlet: I guess.

Rosencrantz (*after a pause*): I mean, it just seems like you're angry about something. I don't know. It probably won't help to keep it bottled up inside if you're mad at us. Just tell us if you're angry.

Hamlet: I just feel…powerless.

Rosencrantz: You? Powerless? You're the prince of Denmark and next in line for the throne!

Hamlet: So? Ever hear of a gilded cage?

Enter Actors playing Recorders poorly

Hamlet: Oooh. Music. Lemme see one of those things. (*takes recorder and badly plays Hot Cross Buns*) Remember that diddy? Heh. Good times. What does it matter to you guys if I'm angry or not?

III.II

Guildenstern: I mean, you're our bro, dude.

Hamlet: Is that a fact? Huh. How's about you play a lil something on this for us?

Guildenstern: Uh…I don't know how.

Hamlet: Aw, c'mon. You're my bro after all. You'd never do anything to hurt me or betray me, right?

Guildenstern: Of course not. But…I still don't know how to play.

Hamlet: It's just as easy as lying. All you do is put your fingers here and blow into it. And then you got music! Easy!

Guildenstern: Yeah, I understand the concept, but I still don't know how to play it.

Hamlet: You guys must not think much of me then. You can't even play a song on a shitty little recorder and here you are trying to play a song on me. Do you think I was born yesterday? I know everything I tell you will be repeated the king and queen. You won't be getting anything out of me, bro.

Enter Polonius

Polonius: My prince, I must stress that the queen wants to speak with you post haste!

Hamlet (*squinting toward sky*) Does that cloud look like a camel?

Polonius: Why, yes, I believe it does.

Hamlet: (*looking at Rosencrantz or Guildenstern*) Or maybe it looks like a weasel.

Polonius: Yes, I suppose it does appear weaselly.

III.II

Hamlet (*slapping Polonius' belly*): Actually, I think it looks more like a whale.

Polonius: Oh ho ho. Yes, I see the whale, too.

Hamlet: Well, I suppose I should go see my mother.

Polonius: Yes, that would be a good idea.

Hamlet: I'll be there in a minute.

Exit Polonius

Hamlet: Everyone get out of here. I need time to brood.

Exit everyone but Hamlet.

Hamlet: I can feel it in the air. Something is coming. I don't know what it is yet, but I can feel it welling up. And now my mother wants to see me. I gotta go in there and find out what she knows, if she had any part to play in Papa's murder. I gotta be as cold as ice. I gotta work my tongue like a dagger. It's the only way I'll know the truth.

Exit Hamlet

Scene III

King's Throne Room.
King, Rosencrantz, and Guildenstern are sitting around.

King: Hamlet has gone frooty-loops and I don't like it one bit. We are strictly a Frosted Flakes family. It's not safe for the prince to be running around shooting off his mouth and spreading fake news. Rosenboop and Gigglestooge, you two need to get him out of here. Take him somewhere rainy with disgusting food and butt-ugly people.

Guildenstern: …You mean England?

King: Yes! Perfect! Take him there until we can figure out what's going on.

Rosencrantz: Welp, considering you'll throw us in jail and torture us if we don't do what you say, consider it done!

King: That's what I like to hear. I wish you three a safe voyage. It would be so sad if you were attacked and murdered by pirates on the way to England by accident. Now go on and get outta here!

Exit Rosencrantz and Guildenstern

Enter Polonius

Polonius: Your grace, the prince is going to the Queen's chambers. I'm going to hide behind the curtains and eavesdrop. This seems like a good idea even though the prince is unstable and has recently taken to carrying a sword around. I will tell you everything I hear when they're finished. Shouldn't be more than five or ten minutes. Anyways, see you again real soon, definitely

King: Yeah, okay, whatever.

III.III

Exit Polonius

King: Hoooooo boy. I am in way over my head. Everyone is going to find out what I did and that I have absolutely no idea what I'm doing. There's got to be some way to make all of this go away. I could pin the blame on someone else. Maybe get a few of my advisors to resign, send a few more to jail? Maybe that will throw them all off the trail... Ah, but what's the use in that? I was the one who sold my soul. I was the one who poured the ear poison. And now the prince is hot on my trail. I was so careful! I'm a very stable genius and I know more than any general in Denmark and this crazy little weirdo is on to me. (*crying*) I just wanted to be king! I just wanted everyone to like me and kick all those dirty immigrants out of my country! Now everyone is going to hate me when they find out I lied and cheated and committed treason to get to where I am. (*Sniffs*) It's okay. The two idiots will take care of the prince and everything will be all better and then everyone will love me and I'll make Denmark great again!

Enter Hamlet

Hamlet: Are you crying?

King: (*wiping eyes*) What? Me? No! Shut up, you're crying.

Hamlet (*staring him down for a long time*): ...Okay. Well...I'm going to go see my mom. (*aside*) I know what you did, you motherfucker.

King: What was that?

Hamlet: Nothing.

Exit Hamlet

King: The sooner that gloomy little twerp goes to England, the

73

III.III

(King cont.)
better.

Exit King

Scene IV

**Queen's Room. It resembles a suite in the 3rd best hotel/casino in Atlantic City thirty years ago.
Queen and Polonius are standing around.**

Polonius: The prince is on his way. You need to be firm with him, but not too firm. Tell him this gloominess needs to stop and that we're all at wits end with his craziness. Don't forget to let him know that the King is very concerned about his behavior and that something bad might happen to him if he doesn't straighten up. Considering you're a woman, you still need male supervision so I'll just hide behind this curtain because that seems like a totally reasonable thing to do around a paranoid and dangerous cretin with a sword.

Hamlet (*off stage*): Mom?

Queen: Okay, shut up, he's coming. Get in your spot.

Polonius hides behind curtain.

Enter Hamlet

Hamlet: You wanted to see me?

Queen: Yes. You really upset your father today.

Hamlet: You've really upset my father.

Queen: Really, Gus, er Hamlet, don't you take that tone with me.

Hamlet: Don't take that tone with me, you bitch.

Queen (*shocked*): Hamlet!

Hamlet (*bored*): What is it now?

III.IV

Queen: I'm not one of your little friends. Did you forget who you're talking to?

Hamlet: No, I remember. You're the queen. Your dead husband's brother's wife. And unfortunately, you're also my mother.

Queen: If that's how you're going to speak to me, then I'll let your father deal with you and I have a feeling you won't like how he handles your sass.

Queen starts toward door.

Hamlet blocks her exit.

Hamlet (*drawing sword*): No, you're not going anywhere. Not until you admit what you did to Papa.

Queen (*afraid*): You raise your sword to your own mother? Please, Hamlet, you're not thinking clearly! (*calling out*) Help! Help!

Polonius (*still behind curtain*): Help! Help! The queen is in danger!

Hamlet: What's this? A rat that needs killing? Snitches get stiches! Take this! Yeet! (*stabs through curtain*)

Polonius (*comes stumbling out*): Gah! I'm stabbed! This is it for me. I'm definitely dead. Who could have seen this coming? Ah! (*makes a big show of dying and eventually falls down dead*)

Queen: Hamlet, what have you done?

Hamlet: Looks like I just killed a rat.

Queen: Oh, my son, this is a terrible and bloody sin.

Hamlet: Almost as big of sin as killing a king and marrying his

III.IV

(Hamlet cont.)
brother.

Queen: Killing a king?

Hamlet: That's what I said. (*kicks Polonius*) You big dumb idiot. Welp, looks like this is the last time you'll be sticking your fat nose where it doesn't belong. (*Turns to Queen*) I thought you were better than this, Mother. Spying on your own son. Sit down. We're going to have a talk.

Queen: What have I done for you to treat me this way?

Hamlet: What have you done? Well, let's look at the facts. You pretend to be innocent and modest and turn around and make a mockery of your marriage vows. You pretend to be sweet and devout and religious, but underneath you are a twisted beast. A monster.

Queen: What do you mean? How am I a monster?

Hamlet: You had the world in the palm of your hand. A kind and caring soul, strong, just, and wise. This was the man you married first. And then, you threw it all away. Your new husband poisons his brother and steals the throne for himself. Are you blind? Don't call it lust, either. You're no spring chicken and love doesn't blind you like it does young people. You never stopped to question about the strange and mysterious circumstances of my father's death? You never thought it weird that he just dropped dead? What do you have to say for yourself? I can't help but think that you had something to do with all of this. You could have stopped all of this from happening, but you did nothing because you don't care. Where is your shame? You could have stopped an incompetent and treasonous man from sitting at the helm of our country, but you did nothing. Worse, you put yourself in a position to do what was best for you at the cost of everyone else. What do you have to say?

Queen: Stop it! Shut up!

III.IV

Hamlet: How does it feel taking him to bed every night? Having that sweaty body flopping around on top of you in the same bed you once shared with my father?

Queen (*crying*): Stop it Hamlet! You're killing your mother! Stop it!

Hamlet: A murderer and a villain. He's not one twentieth of my father. He only cares about himself and will run this country straight into the ground. And you're an accomplice to this crime. You're letting it all happen.

Queen: Please…

Hamlet: A buffoon for a king…

Enter Ghost

Hamlet (*to Ghost*): Stand over me, Father and guard me! What would you have me do with your adulterous wife?

Queen: You've gone crazy, Hamlet!

Hamlet: I know what you've done and I will ensure that you will pay the price for your sins.

Ghost: Don't forget your mission Hamlet. Your mother is to be spared. Talk to her, my son. She can still be saved.

Hamlet: Got it. (*To Queen*) What do you have to say for yourself?

Queen: There's nobody there, Hamlet. Who are you talking to?

Hamlet: My Father! Look at him! He's right there, plain as day. Don't pretend you can't see him. Or have you already forgotten the face of your first husband?

III.IV

Queen: I don't see anybody.

Hamlet: You don't?

Queen: Nothing but air.

Hamlet: Then who do you think is talking?

Queen: I don't know. There's nobody here but me and you... and Polonius.

Hamlet: Look! There he goes! You can't see him at all?

Exit Ghost

Queen: You're not well, my son. You're sick, but we can help you. This madness has taken over your brain.

Hamlet: Madness? This is not madness. I am not sick. My heart is beating just fine. And even if I am crazy, there is no denying you need to lay down your sins, Mother. The corruption will rot you from the inside out. Confess and repent. You still have a chance to make things right.

Queen: Hamlet, you're breaking my heart.

Hamlet: Then throw away the shitty half and keep the good one. Go to sleep, but not in my uncle's bed. I hope you're better than this. Stay away from that monster. Cut him off from you. Then it will be that much easier to rid this menace from our country. I beg you, Mother. (*Motions to Polonius' corpse*) I do feel badly about him and hope that heaven will forgive me of my sin. He was a fool, but a good man. In any case, good night. I'm not doing all of this for fun. I wouldn't be acting this way if I didn't think I had to. I'm just trying to do what I think is right and I think the worst is yet to come. And there's one thing I need you to do.

III.IV

Queen: What is it?

Hamlet: In addition to cutting off my Uncle, I need you to tell him that I was never crazy. This entire time I've only be pretending in order to find out the truth of my father's murder. Tell him that. He'll believe it coming from you.

Queen: There is no way I will tell him any of that. You killed someone, Hamlet!

Hamlet: …You know he's sending me to England, right?

Queen: Yes…I have heard that mentioned

Hamlet: Yeah. I know that Rosencrantz and Guildenstern are supposed to "convince" me to go with them. I thought they were my bros, but it's clear that you guys got your hooks in them, either through greed or fear. But I'm already two steps ahead of them, so I'm not really worried about any of that. However, (*motioning to Polonius*) there's no way I'm going to be allowed to stay here when word gets out about this guy. I'll take him into the other room. At least now he's found a way to finally shut up. (*To Polonius*) Let's go, big guy. (*To Queen*) Goodnight, Mother.

Exit Hamlet, dragging Polonius' body out with him.

III.IV

Act IV

The Subtle Art of Diplomacy and Subterfuge

Scene I

**The King's Throne Room.
King, Queen, Rosencrantz and Guildenstern are doing their respective thangs.**

King sits on throne reading a newspaper. Queen sighs loudly 3 times. Each time, King looks over his newspaper and stares at Queen, waiting for her to start talking. Finally, on the 3rd time, he closes his newspaper. Rosencrantz and Guildenstern are standing around flipping coins.

King: Is something wrong? You've been sitting here sighing for the past twenty minutes. I can't even concentrate on my Peanuts. You know how I get when I don't get my Snoopy. What's the matter? Where's your son?

Queen (*Looking at Rosencrantz and Guildenstern*): I need to speak with the king. (*after several moments of them not understanding*) Alone.

Exit Rosencrantz and Guildenstern mumbling apologies.

Queen: My king, you won't believe what happened to me earlier.

King: What is it, Gertrude? How's Hamlet?

Queen: He's crazier than a rabbit on speed. We were talking in my room when he whipped out his sword, screamed "snitches get stitches", and stabbed Polonius through the curtain.

King: (*trying not to laugh*) Really? No way! So, Polonius is dead, then? It looks like I owe Marcelleus twenty bucks...

Queen: It's not funny, this is serious!

King: Yes (*clears through*) well, I suppose you're right. This

IV.I

(King cont.)
means that the prince is clearly a danger to himself and others. What should we do? We can lock him up in the dungeons until the craziness clears up. Where is he right now?

Queen: He won't stop crying over the body. It seems like he feels pretty bad about the whole thing.

King: Okay, that's it. We can't deal with this craziness any longer. He's too dangerous to be swinging his sword around here in Denmark. Let's pawn him off on someone else for a while until the heat dies down. Hey, Rogglestoop, Gudenstore! Get back in here!

Enter Rosencrantz and Guildenstern

King: Okay, you idiots. Listen close: The prince has murdered Polonius and for whatever reason won't leave the body. Go find him and bring the corpse into the chapel before it starts stinking up the joint. You understand? Go! Now!

Exit Rosencrantz and Guildenstern

King: Come along, Gertrude. We have the best people to talk to. Simply the best, ain't that right, folks? They're so smart, we'll tell them all about my genius plan and they'll know that we've got everything under control and that the country isn't being undermined by incompetence, insanity, and treason. Let's go!

Scene II

A room in the castle.

Enter Hamlet

Hamlet: (*clapping dust from hands*) Okay, body is…buried.

Rosencrantz and Guildenstern (*off stage*): Hamlet! Dude?

Enter Rosencrantz and Guildenstern

Rosencrantz: Dude, where's Polonius' body?

Hamlet: I buried it.

Guildenstern: Where? We'll dig it up and bring it to the church to bury it again later.

Hamlet: Don't believe it.

Rosencrantz: Don't believe what?

Hamlet: Don't believe that I'll listen to whatever you two dumb fucks say. You've got as much spine and brainpower between you as a sponge and you're gonna try to order around the son of a king? Haha. I don't think so.

Guildenstern: I'm a sponge?

Hamlet: That's right, a big nasty soggy sponge soaking up the king's orders, riches, and butt-sweat. It makes sense though because he's the kind of king to keep mindless yes-men like you around since you make him feel like a big man with the way you let him order you around. But don't worry, when the shit hits the fan he'll throw you under the bus once you outlive your usefulness.

IV.II

Rosencrantz: Dude, what are you talking about?

Hamlet: I didn't think you'd understand. You guys are too stupid to even be insulted.

Guildenstern: Yeah, well, we still need to know where the body is.

Hamlet: The body is with the king, but the king isn't with the body. The king is a thing.

Rosencrantz: The king is a thing?

Hamlet: It doesn't matter. Take me to him. Let's get this over with.

Exit all.

Scene III

The King's Throneroom.

Enter King with Servants

King: I'm going to start calling the prince Crazy Hammy. He's completely lost his marbles. Sad! I've sent our best men after him to find the body of Polonius. I'm so smart. Everyone is so happy that I'm such a tremendous leader. Isn't that right everyone, aren't you just thrilled? Denmark is going to be a fabulous country after we've sent Crazy Hammy away. Everyone is going to be so tired of winning.

Servants nod and fawn over King like a bunch of toadies. Some look a little reluctant but toe the line anyway.

Enter Rosencrantz

King: And here's the man now. Let's hear the good news, Roddlecrow.

Rosencrantz: Well…you see..the thing is…he won't tell us.

King: Where is he?

Rosencrantz: He's waiting right outside.

King: Send him in!

Rozencrantz (*calling off stage*): Bring him in!

Enter Guildenstern and Hamlet

King: Okay, son. Where's Polonius?

Hamlet: At dinner.

IV.III

King: At dinner? Where?

Hamlet: Well, he's not eating dinner. He is dinner…for the worms, just like how everyone else will eventually be worm food. Doesn't matter if you're a beggar or a king, the worms will eat you just the same.

King: Oh boy…

Hamlet: It's funny because a man can fish with a worm that's eaten a king and then eat the fish that's eaten that worm. It's almost as if it's some kind of circular representation of life.

King: What are you talking about?

Hamlet: Nothing. Just trying to remind you that one day a king might become poor people shit.

King: That's enough of that. Where's Polonius?

Hamlet: In heaven. If your messengers can't find him there, I'll be willing to bet you'd be able to personally find him in hell yourself. If you're trying to find him sooner, you can start by checking the flowerbed in the courtyard.

King (*to servants*): Grab a shovel and start digging up the flower-bed.

Hamlet: He'll be waiting for you there.

Exit Servants

King: Listen, Cra- Son. You broke the law when you murdered Polonius. If you were just a commoner, we'd probably just chop your head off and be done with it. Since you're the Prince, we're just going to keep this quiet and send you off somewhere safe until the heat dies down.

IV.III

Hamlet: To England, right?

King: Yep, that's the place.

Hamlet: All right.

King: That's it? Wow, I'm a better negotiator than I thought! I'm glad you understand.

Hamlet: Yep. It's fine. Goodbye, mother!

King: You mean father?

Hamlet: No, I mean mother. Since father and mother is man and wife and through marriage man and wife are one flesh by the transitive property you're my mother. Anyways, off to England!

Exit Hamlet

King (*to Rosencrantz and Guildenstern*): You two make sure the prince doesn't get lost along the way. Get him on that boat as soon as possible. Go on, go!

Exit Rosencrantz and Guildenstern

King: Okay, England. Let's hope you do your job and make sure the Prince doesn't come back. If only terrible food and rain were deadly in high doses. He'd be a goner in a second. To be safe, I think I'll go through with my plan of adding a little insurance by paying some pirates to accidently attack the Prince's ship completely at random. This letter should do the trick. Then once Crazy Hammy is dead and gone it should be smooth sailing from here on out.

IV.IV

Scene IV

A field in Denmark.

Enter Fortinbras with his Captain and his Army

Fortinbras: Okay, go on and tell the Danish King that we're marching through his kingdom and are definitely not going to try to kill him in the exact same way my father was killed. If he gets all uppity, just compliment the size of his hands and he should settle down.

Captain: Yes, Sir!

Fortinbras: Godspeed, soldier.

Exit all but Captain

Enter Hamlet, Rosencrantz, Guildenstern, and attendants.

Hamlet: Woah, what have we got here? Where are you guys coming from?

Captain: Norway, sir.

Hamlet: What's a Norwegian army doing all the way out here?

Captain: We are marching against the…Polish?

Hamlet: Ah, yes, I see. And who is leading this charge?

Captain: That would be Fortinbras, nephew to Fortinbras.

Hamlet: Oh really? My dad murdered a guy name Fortinbras on the battlefield once. I wonder if they're related…Anyways, are you marching to Poland's capital or are you going to the frontier?

Captain: In truth, we're actually marching for this shitty little patch

IV.IV

(Captain cont.)
of grass on the Danish border that has no strategic or monetary value for Poland. Can't imagine why we would ever want to set up an army there if we were attacking the Polish. Now, if we were attacking the Danish…

Hamlet: So, the Polish probably won't even defend it then.

Captain: Nope. We've actually already got troops there honoring the sacred tradition of "squatter's rights".

Hamlet: All right. Well, good luck with your shitty patch of grass then.

Captain: Bye.

Exit Captain.

Rosencrantz: Can we keep moving, please, my lord?

Hamlet: I'll be right there. I want to do a little brooding out here in the fresh air.

Exit all but Hamlet

Hamlet: All signs are pointing me toward revenge. What's the point of being alive if all we do is eat and sleep like animals? We have this gift of wisdom and higher knowledge and what do we do with it? In most of us, it's completely wasted. The worst part is that some of us know the right thing to do and are too cowardly to step up and do it. Everything around me is pointing me in the direction of what I know I need to do. It's saying "you have the cause and the will and the strength and the means to do it." Like this army. It's strong and powerful and led by a delicate and tender prince who has ambition and strength. He's willing to face the unknown, to face death and uncertainty for fortune, for even just a shitty patch of Polish grass. This is greatness. This is true honor.

IV.IV

(Hamlet cont.)
If he can face down death for basically nothing, what about me? I have a murdered father, a corrupted mother, and just cause to take my revenge and what do I do? I let it lie. Twenty thousand men march and are willing to lay down their lives for nothing. I need to be stronger. I need to take my revenge or I'm worth less than nothing.

Scene V

**The King's Throne Room.
The Queen is seated in her throne and Horatio standing before her.**

Queen: Ugh…do I have to talk to her?

Horatio: I think talking to a strong female role model like yourself would really help her out.

Queen: What's the matter with her?

Horatio: Well, she won't stop talking about her dad, who, as you know, was murdered by your son, her boyfriend. She keeps talking about hearing things and attacking the furniture. She can't form a coherent sentence without going off and rambling in a million directions. She's snapped and completely forgotten what it means to be a lady. She needs your help, my queen.

Queen: Ugh, fine. Send her in.

Exit Horatio

Queen (*shaking head*): The things I do for this country…I can't help but feel like I'm partly responsible for all of this.

Enter Horatio and Ophelia

Ophelia: Where's the queen?

Queen: Over here, Ophelia!

Ophelia (*singing*): Some-body once told me the world was gonna roll me…I ain't the sharpest tool in the shed…

Queen: My sweet girl, what inspired you to sing such a beautiful

IV.V

(Queen cont.)
song?

Ophelia: Not a Shrek fan? Okay, that's fine. Here's an Ophelia Original. (*Sings to the tune of The Times are A'changing*)
>Come Senators, Congressmen, please heed the call,
>Come learn of the story of an idiot's fall
>Hiding behind a curtain and blinds
>This moron was stabbed about four or five times!

Queen: Very nice, Ophelia. Now come sit down so we can talk-

Ophelia: Hold on, we're getting to the good part. (*sings*)
>This is what happens when you're dumb as a stone

Enter King and Attendants

Queen: Check this out, my king.

Ophelia (*singing*): Your life ends up wa-sted.

King: How are you today, beautiful?

Ophelia: Hello good sir! Are you satisfied with your long-distance plan? I certainly am! We know what we are and what we are is nothing! I hope God joins you for dinner tonight.

King: I'm sorry to hear about your dad.

Ophelia: Don't even worry about it! Here's another Ophelia Original: (*Sings to the tune of Life on Mars?*)

>It's a god-awful small affair
>To the maid with the golden hair
>While she's climbing in your window
>And she's taking off all of her clothes
>And her friend is locking the door

IV.V

(**Ophelia cont.**)
>She came through the window pure
>Fresh with the morning dew
>She ain't leaving that way no more…

King: Great song!

Ophelia: Thank you, thank you. Let's bring it home! (*Sings to the tune of Eight Days a Week*)

>I heard you said you loved me,
>I guess I thought it true.
>You told me that you loved me.
>And I needed you.
>But now you're gone.
>I don't know what to do.
>I need you, badly.
>I can't live without you.

King: How long has she been like this?

Ophelia: Thank you, thank you. Super excited to be here performing at Madison Square Garden! I want to dedicate this performance to my late father, who's going to be put to bed one last time. I also want to give a quick shout-out to my brother, Laertes! I love you, you syphilitic moron! Finally, I want to thank you, the audience. (*gestures to crowd*) You're a beautiful audience. (*Bows*) Good night to all, and to all a good night!

Exit Ophelia

King: Hmmm….Someone should keep an eye on her and make sure she doesn't break any of my stuff. (*Stares at Horatio*)

Exit Horatio.

King: Well, it's clear what's going on here, isn't it folks? Ophelia

IV.V

(King cont.)
is suffering from grief madness in the wake of her father's death. Gertrude my love, isn't it so true that when sorrows come, they never come alone. First, Polonius croaks, then we send Crazy Hamlet away, which, let's be honest here, was completely his own fault. Luckily, we'll keep this quiet, even if the tabloids are whispering about a cover up. We've done the right thing by sending the prince away. Poor Ophelia simply couldn't handle the pressure and snapped. What she doesn't know is that her brother is back from France and has been observing our country's proud tradition of drinking, whoring, and ignoring objective fact by pretending his father isn't dead. This is a mess, my queen. And only I can fix it.

A ruckus ensues off stage.

Queen: Did you hear something?

King: It was probably nothing. In any case…Guards! Block the door!

Attendants start to lock the door but stop.

Enter Courier

King: What is it now?

Courier (*panting for breath*): My…my king…(*still panting*)…My king…(*struggling for air*)

King: Yes? What is it? We don't have all day.

Courier: (*catches breath*) It's Laertes, your grace. He's back and he's sober! And he's angry. He's got a following of people who want him to be king and he's coming right now!

Queen: An illegitimate king! Who would do such a thing?

IV.V

More ruckus off stage.

King: Hoo-boy…uh, it sounds like he's breaking in!

Enter Laertes holding a sword with Soldiers at his back.

Laertes: Where is the king? Stand down, men.

Soldier: We need to protect you, my lord! Who is going to start the fire that burns this whole place down if you die?

Laertes: I got this, guys. Go guard the door to make sure we aren't interrupted.

Soldier: Yes, sir!

Soldiers exit to guard door.

Laertes: Thank you. Now, Claudius, you rat, where is my father?

Queen: Calm down, Laertes. We don't want to do anything rash.

Laertes: Calm down? Calm down?? Don't you tell me to calm down! My father is dead and someone is going to pay for it!

King: Okay, Laertes, what's the matter? Don't worry Gertrude, there's nothing to fear. God protects kings from treason. Okay, Laertes, let's hear it, let him go Gertrude. Speak.

Laertes: Where is my dad?

King: …He's dead.

Queen: But the King had nothing to do with it!

King: Let Laertes speak!

IV.V

Laertes: How did he die? Give me a straight answer. I know all of your tricks, Claudius, and I won't be fooled by your silver tongue or big brain moves. I don't give a shit if you're the king. If you had anything to do with my father's death, I'll put my sword straight through your heart.

King: You and what army?

Laertes: Did you not see the soldiers ready to burn this whole place down a minute ago?

King: Uh…that won't be necessary. So, Laertes, you're really serious about getting revenge for your father? Like, you'll get revenge no matter who did it?

Laertes: You bet your sweet ass I will. I'll murder the shit out of anyone. You, her (*points at queen*), even an entire audience if I have to!

King: I admire your tenacity, Laertes. It reminds me of a younger, poorer, and uglier version of myself. Now, I'll be honest. I didn't have anything to do with your father's death. I'm being really truly honest here. You can judge for yourself.

Soldiers (*off stage*): Let her through!

Laertes: What is it now?

Enter Ophelia mumbling to herself with drunken, awkward movement

Laertes: Jesus! Ophelia, I told you to stay in your room! Oh, my poor sweet crazy sister. Your brains were all you had and now even those are gone! I promise that I'll get double revenge for you and dad. I'm gonna revenge the shit out of whoever is responsible for this… twice.

IV.V

Ophelia (*singing*):
>Laertes-Laertes, always getting with the ladies.
>It's a shame it's a trick
>that he'll make all them sick,
>poking them all with his syphilis dick.

Laertes: Uh…my poor crazy sister! Even if you totally weren't completely and one hundred percent crazy and talking nonsense, you wouldn't be able to talk me out of this revenge!

Ophelia: No, that's not how the song goes at all. You need to dig deep and really belt it out. Give it another try. Take it from the top!

Laertes: Uh...

Ophelia: I see. You need something to get you going. It's totally normal and happens to tons of men. I think I might have something here to help you with your little problem. You don't have a heart condition, right?

Laertes: My poor crazy sister.

Ophelia: (*searching herself for something*): No, seriously. I've got them right here. Well, I had them. Pop one of these little blue guys and you'll be right as rain. You'll be larger than life when I'm through with you. You got real star power, kid and with my help we're gonna be taking you straight to the top of the charts. That's one way to make the old man proud. I remember I was on track to be a singer myself, but then my dad croaked and put a wrench straight in the works.

Laertes: Okay, Ophelia, I think it's time to go. Uh…you're wanted on set in five minutes.

Ophelia: Five minutes? I haven't even done my warm-ups. Oh, my agent is going to hear about this. (*Singing*)
>Oh Polonius,

IV.V

>
> **(Ophelia cont.)**
> Stupid Polonius.
> You went and threw it all away.
> Behind the curtain
> You were hurtin',
> When you were stabbed yesterday.
> Oh Polonius
> Stupid Polonius
> We miss you now that you're gone
> One piece of relief
> In all of this grief
> Is we can't hear you blabber on.

Okay, I'm warmed up. Adieu! (*Bows*)

Exit Ophelia

Laertes: Jesus, do you see what I'm working with here?

King: Laertes, nobody knows better than I do about how you're feeling. I am so, so sorry about your dead dad and your crazy sister. I'm gonna make you a deal. You talk to all of your smartest friends, besides me that is, and if they find any evidence that I had anything to do with your father's death, I will give you my kingdom, my crown, and even my life. If they don't find anything, then all I ask in return is your patience in this matter. We will help you find the true killer.

Laertes: I mean…you have to admit, the fact that his death and burial were kept secret and there was no funeral or any kind of rites given, seems pret-ty suspicious.

King: You make a good point. And all I'll say is that the great axe will fall on whoever is responsible. Come with me. I want to talk to you in the other room.

Exit King and Laertes

Scene VI

A different room in the castle.
Horatio and Servant enter.

Horatio: Ugh what's that goddawful smell? I thought they buried Polonius already.

Servant: Yes, well, that smell is actually coming from the other room. There are some sailors here to see you. I couldn't really understand them, but I think they want to speak with you.

Horatio: You couldn't just take a message?

Servant: They were pretty…insistent that they speak only to you directly.

Horatio: Fine, whatever, send 'em in.

Exit Servant

Horatio: This must have something to do with Hamlet. He's the only one who would send a message like this from halfway across the world.

Enter Sailors

Sailor: Yous Horatios?

Horatio: Regrettably, yes.

Sailor: Here yas goes. (*Hands Horatio letter*)

Horatio: Thanks

Sailor stands with his hand out and clears his throat.

IV.VI

Horatio (*rolling his eyes*): All right, all right, keep your shirt on.

Horatio drops coins in sailor's hand

Horatio opens and reads letter out loud.

Horatio (*reading*): "Dear Horatio, Please take these sailors to see the king as soon as possible. I know they probably stink, but that's what spending six months on a boat will do to you. We were attacked by pirates two days into our trip to England and they took me hostage. Aside from all the murdering and stealing, they're actually pretty nice guys. Make sure the king gets these letters, then come see me as fast as you can. I've seen some crazy shit these past few days. Rosencrantz and Guildenstern are still heading to England. Dude, you won't believe half of the stuff I'm going to tell you. See you real soon. Your bro, Hamlet."

Well shit…all right guys, you heard the letter. Let's get these papers to the king and then you need to take me back to see Hamlet.

Exit all

Scene VII

**A *different* different room in the castle.
King and Laertes enter**

King: Listen, Laertes, you know that I'm your friend here, right? You need to trust me. I didn't kill your father.

Laertes: Okay…but tell me this: why didn't you punish the guy for his crime?

King: Well…it's kind of complicated. See, his mother's the queen and she simply wouldn't be able to stand seeing her little baby boy suffer and to tell you the truth, I just don't have the heart to hurt the queen myself. Then there's the fact all the people in the kingdom love him and that they'll be pretty upset if we chop his head off.

Laertes: So, my dad is dead and my sister's gone crazy and that gloomy little twerp, Hamlet, gets off scot free?

King: You know, they say you should only worry about things you can control, so… (*leans in conspiratorially*) Listen, don't tell anyone I said this, but your father was actually a pretty okay guy and I guess on some level we were kind of sort of maybe friends. I guess once someone helps you bury a dead stripper they-

Enter Messenger

King: Oh! News! What do you got for me?

Messenger: Letter here from Hamlet. This is for you, your grace, and this one is for the queen.

King: From Hamlet? Who brought them?

Messenger: Some sailors. I dunno, I didn't see them for myself. That guy Horatio sent it along.

IV.VII

King: Okay. Get outta here.

Exit Messenger.

Laertes starts to leave.

King (*stops Laertes from leaving*): No, not you. (*Opens letter*) Let's see what we've got here. (*Reading like someone who is barely literate*): Dear Uncle-Dad. I'm on my way back to Denmark. I would really like to see you. You won't believe what happened to me. See you real soon. Hamlet. (*Looks up from letter*) What does this mean? Are they coming back or is this some kind of joke?

Laertes: Can you recognize the handwriting?

King: Oh, it's Hamlet's, that's for sure. And look at this, there's a PS. (*reading*) PS: Come alone and unarmed. No cops. (*looks up*) What do you think that means?

Laertes: I don't know. It could mean anything. But let him come. I'm looking forward to seeing him in person so I can return the favor he did for my dad.

King: Okay, Laertes. Let me ask you this. How are you going to make this happen? Are you not going to follow the wishes of your king?

Laertes: Well, you don't need to put me in a position to disobey your wishes…

King: Okay, well, listen. I can't have you murdering the prince for no reason. But today's your lucky day because I'm gonna cut you a deal. But you gotta work with me.

Laertes: Really? Man, that would be so much easier than staging a coup and killing you and your wife.

IV.VII

King: Uh…yeah. You know, Hamlet was pretty jealous of you, Laertes.

Laertes: Oh really? Why is that?

King: Well, he was jealous of all the travelling you were able to do, but specifically because you met a particularly special Frenchman. He was a gentleman of Normandy. In spite of being French, he was a fearless warrior that people said was gifted with supernatural abilities.

Laertes (*trying to remember*): A Norman? Are you sure his name wasn't Norman?

King: No, he was a Norman.

Laertes: Oh! I know! Lamond!

King: That's the one!

Laertes: Oh yeah! I remember him! Nice guy. Beautiful daughters-

King: Well, he happens to be a very good friend of mine. And he spoke very highly of you. "Oh, Laertes is the best at sword fighting! Simply the best sword fighter around and everyone knows it!" Well, Hamlet got so jealous that he wanted to see you immediately to prove to he could match your abilities. His mother talked him out of it because the kid is one of the worst swordsman ever. No question. Simply the worst. People say it all the time! "Hamlet is the worst swordsman around."

Laertes: Where are you going with this?

King: Do you want to avenge your father or not?

Laertes: Of course, I do.

IV.VII

King: Well, listen. I know a thing or two about killing people and let me say this: the longer you go without getting revenge, the more likely you'll move on with your life and give up the dream. Don't waste your time. Take advantage of today and make your dreams come true by murdering the guy who killed your dad!

Laertes: Yeah! Okay! How do you plan on making my dream reality?

King: Okay...well, what we can do is just pretend we're having a friendly duel. Nothing crazy. Just first to blood to give everyone a chance to place some bets on you two. Except...something could go terribly wrong and Hamlet could accidentally die!

Laertes: I'll do you one better. When I was abroad, I met this girl who threatened to blackmail...uh...well, it's not important why I have it, but I've got some crazy-strong poison and I can dip my blade in that and can use that to slice the prince with. It'll definitely kill him.

King: I like it. And it might be good to have a plan B. The prince is wire-y and not to say that I don't think you could beat him in a sword fight, but it might be good to use some of that poison on his drink, so that when he takes a water break during the duel, we can just poison him then.

Enter Queen

King: Uh...anyways, so that's how you cure homelessness, Laertes. Oh, hello my queen!

Queen: Hey, Laertes. I've got some more bad news for you. Ophelia drowned to death.

Laertes: What? How?

Queen: She fell underwater and couldn't breathe any air. You

IV.VII

(Queen cont.)
know, she was never much to look at in life, but she was kind of pretty there at the bottom of the river. She almost looked like a mermaid or something.

Laertes: She's dead...?

Queen: Yup.

Laertes: Well, Ophelia's already had too much water, so I won't cry for her. I'm not crying. I'm not crying at all. You're crying!

Laertes runs away crying.

King: Welp. We better track him down before he trips and cracks his head open and ruins my beautiful marble floor.

Exit King and Queen.

Act V

Funeral for a Mermaid

Scene I

**A graveyard outside of the Castle.
Two Gravediggers are perfecting their craft of being drunk and digging holes.**

Gravedigger 1: So, are they giving her a Christian burial or what?

Gravedigger 2: That's what they're saying, yeah. King's orders.

Gravedigger 1: How're we giving her a Christian burial? Did she drown in self-defense?

Gravedigger 2: That's what the king said, yes.

Gravedigger 1: Heh. More like self-offense. If I choose to drown myself, I've made a choice to act and everyone knows action has three parts: to act, to do, and to perform, so clearly she drowned herself willingly.

Gravedigger 2: (*sighs*) Man, I'm getting real sick of this shit from you...

Gravedigger 1: Hear me out! Here's the water. Here's a person. If they go into the water and drowns themself, they choose, they lose, they're going to Hell. But if the water comes to them and drowns them, they haven't done anything wrong.

Gravedigger 2: So, what are you saying? That she didn't choose to drown herself?

Gravedigger 1: Well, the King decreed that she was to be given a Christian burial...

Gravedigger 2: Listen, you and I both know that if it were one of us, they'd toss our body in a ditch before lunch. The only reason

V.I

(Gravedigger 2 cont.)
we're doing this is because she was Polonius' daughter.

Gravedigger 1: Yes, and it's such a shame that the wealthiest and most powerful among us are so sad that they feel the need to hang and drown themselves, while us poor wretches have to wait for sickness or war to kill us to get to heaven. Whatever. At least we have the honor of holding Adam's profession.

Gravedigger 2: Adam was a grave digger?

Gravedigger 1: Yep. Just like you or me.

Gravedigger 2: For who? Whose grave was he digging?

Gravedigger 1: C'mon man, you never read the bible? The bible says 'Adam digg'd'. He wasn't just digging for no reason. He was digging a grave. For who? Well, I've got a few theories on that…

Gravedigger 2: Where? Where does it say that in the Bible?

Gravedigger 1 (*ignoring*): Lemme ask you another question. Who's a better builder than a mason, shipbuilder, or carpenter?

Gravedigger 2: The gallows-maker! That frame outlives a thousand tenants!

Gravedigger 1: Why do you gotta be stepping on my punchlines like that? That's a solid answer, but not what I was thinking. Give it another try.

Gravedigger 2: Hmmm…

Gravedigger 1: It's okay if you're stumped.

Gravedigger 2: I don't know. Who?

V.I

Enter Hamlet and Horatio

Gravedigger 1: Ah, I knew you wouldn't get it. Stop worrying about it or you're gonna hurt yourself. The answer is a grave digger because his houses last until doomsday! (*laughs*) Okay, now why don't you run back and grab us another bottle? I'll finish up here.

Exit Gravedigger 2

Gravedigger 1: (*singing and digging*)
O when I was a boy I loved a girl
Whose hands were very deft
When she touched me, my spirit unfurled
Until I came and left

Hamlet: Does this guy have no respect for the dead? Look at him singing while he digs this grave.

Horatio: Well, think of it this way: to you, this is a very sad occasion, but to him it's just a Tuesday.

Hamlet: I guess. I mean, he could still show a little bit of respect.

Gravedigger 1: (*singing*)
>Age will sneak up on me
>And scoop me in its grasp.
>And that'll be the end of me
>I'll be a thing of the past.

Tosses skull out of the grave

Hamlet: That skull had a tongue in it not long ago and could sing just like he is now. Look at how he's treating it. Tossing it around like a goddamn volleyball. That could have been the skull of someone important like a politician, or a king, or a celebrity.

V.I

Horatio: Yeah, I guess you're right.

Hamlet: Or it could have been the skull of a commoner who says "Good morning, my lord. How are you doing, my lord? Let me wipe your ass, my lord." You know, someone like you, Horatio.

Horatio: Uh…yeah.

Hamlet: I guess it doesn't matter who you are cause one way or another your skull is gonna get knocked around by some drunken idiot's shovel. What's the point of suffering through life if your bones are meant to become a moron's plaything?

Gravedigger 1 (*singing*):
>Picks and shovels and garden spades
>These are how dreams are made.
>Laying down for that final rest,
>I'd lay my head on a maiden's breast!

Tosses another skull

Hamlet: Look at that! Another skull! That could have been a lawyer's skull for all we know. So much for all those brains knocking around in there. Lotta good that did him, huh? I mean, what's even the point-

Horatio (*annoyed*): Listen, if you're so concerned about the grave, why don't you just ask him whose grave it is.

Hamlet: That's a great idea, Horatio! I think I will. (*To Gravedigger*) Excuse me, sir! Whose grave are you digging?

Gravedigger 1 (*without looking away from his work*): Mine.

Hamlet: Yes, it looks like yours, since you're standing in it.

Gravedigger 1: Well, you're standing outside of it, so it's clearly not yours. I'm not gonna be lying in it, but it's definitely mine.

V.I

Hamlet: You're lying in it while you're in it since you're saying it's yours. It's for the dead, not the quick, so you're lying.

Gravedigger 1: It's a quick lie, all right. Now leave me alone, I've got digging to be done.

Hamlet: What man do you dig it for?

Gravedigger 1: For no man, my lord.

Hamlet: Okay, which woman, then?

Gravedigger 1: No woman either.

Hamlet: Jesus dude. Who's supposed to be buried in it?

Gravedigger 1: She used to be a woman, but now she's dead.

Hamlet: This fucking guy. Can you think of a bigger pain in the ass, Horatio? (*to Gravedigger*) How long have you been a gravedigger?

Gravedigger 1: Oh man…I got my start when our dear departed King Hamlet beat Fortinbras. The same year Prince Hamlet was born. Speaking of Prince Hamlet, did you hear that he got sent away to England?

Hamlet (*aside to Horatio*): This guy is so drunk he doesn't even recognize me. (*to Gravedigger*) Why was he sent to England?

Gravedigger 1: Well, he'll fit right in over there with all the other deranged morons. The prince went crazy, you know.

Hamlet: How'd he go crazy?

Gravedigger 1: Well, I can't say for sure, but I've been told the young prince was doing all kinds of disgusting stuff: ritual sacri

V.I

(Gravedigger cont.)
fice, worshipping the devil, eating pizza with no sauce on it.

Hamlet: On what grounds do you make this claim?

Gravedigger 1: Here in Denmark, of course! I've been digging here for oh….30 years.

Hamlet: Okay new subject: how long does it take for a man to rot?

Gravedigger 1: Well, that all depends. Some of the bodies we've been burying are barely staying together when we're putting them in the ground. There's some nasty syphilis going around these days. But if you keep it clean, oh, I'd say six or seven years. A tanner is nine years easy.

Hamlet: Why does it take longer for a tanner to rot?

Gravedigger 1: Well, because of his trade. His skin keeps the water out and since water is what speeds up the process of rotting, he doesn't rot as fast. Here's a skull that's been underground for 23 years. Clean as a whistle.

Hamlet: Whose was it?

Gravedigger 1: Ah, he was a crazy bastard. Who do you think it was?

Hamlet: I don't recognize him.

Gravedigger 1: Died of the plague. Poured a tankard of ale over my head once. That's the skull of Yorik. The king's jester.

Hamlet: It was?

Gravedigger 1: That's what the headstone says.

V.I

Hamlet: Let me see that. (*Takes the skull*) Alas….poor Yorick!

Horatio (*silently mouths, confused*): Alas?

Hamlet: Ah, I knew him Horatio. This guy was the best. When I was little, he would let me ride on his back. It used to be a happy memory, now it makes me sick. Here were once the lips I kissed I don't know how many times.

Horatio looks confused and concerned that Hamlet as a little boy was kissing a grown man on the mouth.

Hamlet (*to skull*): Where are your jokes now? Your songs? All those times you made the whole room laugh. What good did that do for anyone? Maybe if you're in heaven you can go find Ophelia and tell her a joke. (*to Horatio*) Horatio, can I ask you a question?

Horatio: You just did.

Hamlet: Do you think Alexander the Great laid down in the earth like this?

Horatio: I don't know, I never met the guy.

Hamlet: And smelt rotten like this? (*drops the skull*)

Horatio: Uh…probably?

Hamlet: It's crazy that we return to the dust, Horatio. Even some as great as Alexander will eventually be eaten and shit out.

Horatio: It's the circular representation of life, my lord.

Hamlet: Yep. It just blows my mind. Alexander the Great was born. Alexander the Great died. Alexander the Great was buried and returned to the earth. We use the earth to build things. Who's to say part of the Alexander the Great isn't part of our castle or some

V.I

(**Hamlet cont.**)
thing? Oh, shit, here comes the king…

Enter the King, Queen, Laertes, Priest, and attendants with a coffin in a funeral procession.

Hamlet: Man, he's rolling deep. Let's see what they're doing. (*Hides behind a headstone as they come to the grave and lower the coffin into the ground.*)

Hamlet: That's Laertes. What's he doing with them? He's supposed to be in France...

Laertes: Are we going to do anything else for her?

Priest: Well…it's tough considering how she died…Technically we should be burying her upside down and hitting her with sticks and rocks and cursing her to eternal damnation. However, since she was a virgin, we'll give her the usual rites. Plus, the king specifically ordered us to do so.

Laertes: So, there's no other way we can honor her?

Priest: I'm afraid not. We can't profane the services we give to good Christians by giving one to her.

Laertes (*furious*): Profane the services? Put her in the ground and violets will spring from her grave! Listen here, holy man, my sister will be an angel singing in heaven while you're screaming here on Earth. You think I'm afraid to punch a priest? Keep it up and you'll be going to meet God yourself!

Hamlet: What?? Ophelia??

Queen: (*throws flowers*) Sweets to the sweet. So long, Ophelia. You might've only been a four out of ten, but Hamlet would have been lucky to marry you.

V.I

Laertes: Oh, my poor sister. I'm gonna rain down 10 times the pain on the piece of shit that's responsible for this. Don't bury her yet! Let me hug my sister one last time! (*Jumps into the grave*) Just bury us together! I don't want to live without my sister, even if she was kind of uppity.

Hamlet (*approaching*): You call that grieving? I'll show you how to mourn your sister! It's me, Hamlet the Dane! (*Jumps into the grave*)

Laertes: Get out of here, you piece of shit! She was my sister!

The two fight in the grave.

Hamlet: You better get your hands off me, Laertes. I may not look like much, but don't you make me release the beast all over your stupid face.

King: I got five on Laertes! (*waves a dollar*)

Queen: Hamlet! Stop!

Horatio: Hamlet, chill, dude!

Attendants: Stop! Stop!

Attendants break them up.

Hamlet: I'll fight you until my last breath, you syphilitic idiot.

Queen: Why?

Hamlet: I loved Ophelia. Forty thousand brothers couldn't even touch the love I felt for her! What would you do for her?

Laertes: Oh yeah? Well you-

V.I

King (*interrupting Laertes*): Crazy Hammy is crazy, Laertes.

Queen: Hamlet, please! Calm down!

Hamlet: What would you do for her? Would you weep? Fight? Fast? Kill yourself? Drink Gasoline? Eat a crocodile? I'll do all of that. Did you just come here to whine? To show me up by jumping in her grave? Well, if you're getting buried with her, I'll be buried with her too. Let them bury us all under a mountain of dirt! I was the only one who truly loved her.

Laertes: I'll have you know I-

Queen (*interrupting Laertes*): This is crazy. Everyone needs to calm down. We all miss Ophelia, although this is probably the first time two men have ever fought over her…

Hamlet: Listen, I don't know what problem you have with me, Laertes. I thought you and I were bros. But it doesn't matter. I'm ready to go whenever you are. I'm always ready. I'm always watching. Just name the time and the place. **Exits stage staring at Laertes and walking backwards slowly.**

King: Horatio, make sure he doesn't bump into anything. He's still walking backwards.

Exit Horatio.

King: (*To Queen*) My queen, you should go make sure your son is okay. (*Aside to Laertes*) Welp, looks like we've got an excuse for our duel. We'll let things calm down a bit, then go forward with the plan.

Exit all.

Scene II

A room in the Castle
Hamlet and Horatio are sitting at a table.

Hamlet: I guess I should tell you about how I got off the boat, huh?

Horatio: Whatever.

Hamlet: I was trying to fall asleep, but there was something keeping me awake. No... not that. I had made sure to take care of *that* before leaving. It was something else. It was almost like…divine intervention.

Horatio (*flatly*): Fascinating, my lord.

Hamlet: I don't know what compelled me to do it, but I opened the letter that Rosencrantz and Guildenstern were delivering to the King of England from my uncle. And do you want to know what it said?

Horatio: I'm sure you'll tell me regardless…

Hamlet: It was an order to have my head chopped off immediately!

Horatio: Gasp.

Hamlet: Read it for yourself. Do you want to know what I did then?

Horatio: No.

Hamlet: I wrote a new letter. Do you want to know what it said?

Horatio: Not at all.

Hamlet: It was an order to put whoever delivered the letter to

V.II

(Hamlet Cont.)
death. I just so happened to have a copy of the king's seal in my bag, so the note was a perfect forgery. I put it back where I found it and those two idiots were none the wiser.

Horatio: Damn. That's cold-blooded, man. So, Rosencrantz and Guildenstern are dead.

Hamlet: Whatever. They were my uncle's puppets and were willing to fuck me over as if my friendship meant nothing to them. If I didn't kill them off, my uncle would have eventually.

Horatio: What kind of leader would do that?

Hamlet: I don't know. What kind of leader kills his brother and marries his widow? What kind of leader snatches power that he is not entitled to? What kind of leader lies and steals and commits treason for personal gain? And what am I supposed to do about it? Just let him slide and keep plundering my country?

Horatio: You know he's going to find out what you did eventually, right?

Hamlet: That won't matter. Right now, I've got the element of surprise and I'll use it when the time is right. I do feel bad about that whole thing with Laertes. He's an okay guy and I just forgot myself, I guess. I should apologize. I guess I just got worked up about Ophelia…

Horatio: Someone's coming. Who's there?

Enter Osric, who looks strikingly similar to Polonius

Osric: Welcome back to Denmark, my prince.

Hamlet: Thank you. (*aside to Horatio*) Do you know this jabroni?

V.II

Horatio: (*aside to Hamlet*) No.

Hamlet: (*aside to Horatio*) He's got more money than sense. Basically Polonius 2.0. Another windbag idiot. Check this out.

Osric: My prince, if you aren't too busy, the king has requested something for you.

Hamlet: Yes, I will do whatever the king needs. But first, please make sure to wear your hat when you speak to me. It goes on your head.

Osric: (*puts on hat*) Thank you, sir. It is quite hot out here.

Hamlet: Nah, I think it's actually pretty chilly.

Osric: Ah, yes, I misspoke, my lord. Indeed, it is cold.

Hamlet: But it's actually pretty hot for how cold it is. And take off your hat when addressing me.

Osric: Uh...yes...of course my lord. (*takes off hat*) Now, the king has placed a large wager on you...

Hamlet: Hat! (*motions to put on hat*)

Osric: Uh, yes. (*puts on hat*) In any case, Laertes is a fine young gentleman. Perhaps one of the finest and youngest gentleman I've ever had the pleasure to meet.

Hamlet: Yeah, he's okay, I guess. What about him?

Osric: Well, you see, sir....

Hamlet: Spit it out, already.

Osric: I am sure you're aware...

V.II

Hamlet: Get on with it!

Osric: I am sure you're aware that Laertes is excellent…

Hamlet: At having syphilis? Well, yes, of course, everyone knows that.

Osric: No, my lord. He's excellent with a weapon.

Hamlet: Which weapon?

Osric: With the dagger and rapier.

Hamlet: That's two weapons.

Osric: Yes, so it is. In any case, the king has bet six horses against six French swords.

Hamlet: Okay? So what? What does this have to do with me?

Osric: The king has bet that you can beat Laertes in a duel.

Hamlet: And if I refuse?

Osric: Well, you would be refusing an order from your king and we would have to waterboard you.

Hamlet: Hmmm. Sure, why not. What's the worst that can happen?

Horatio: You could get stabbed or-

Osric (*interrupting*): Shall I take you there now?

Hamlet: Give me a second to collect myself.

Osric: Wonderful sir. Thank you.

V.II

Exit Osric

Horatio: That guy sucks.

Hamlet: Yep. Just another of a long line of idiot yes-men for my uncle to boss around to feel important. Lackies like that are the fucking worst. Their blind obedience makes me want to throw up. They don't have an ounce of brains or spine inside of them. It's guys like that let guys like my uncle fuck the whole world up.

Enter a Lord who looks strikingly similar to Osric and Polonius

Hamlet: And here we have another one.

Lord: My prince, the king wants to know if you are coming to duel Laertes or if you need another minute.

Hamlet: Meh, I'll get to it eventually.

Lord: The queen asked me to tell you to take it easy when dueling as she would hate to see you get hurt.

Hamlet: Good advice. It would really suck to die in the middle of a duel, especially with such a bright and promising future ahead of me.

Exit Lord.

Horatio: Dude, there's no way you can win this bet.

Hamlet: Hey, you never know. While he was whoring it up in France, I was studying the blade. I can beat him.

Horatio: I really don't think-

Hamlet: Come onnnn…Lighten up dude. When was the last time anyone got hurt from a little swordplay?

V.II

Horatio: All right man, it's your funeral.

Hamlet: If this is my time to go, it's my time to go. If I somehow manage to get killed in a duel fighting Laertes, then fuck it, I went out like a baller. Maybe if I get killed in a duel, they'll write a hit Broadway play about me that'll win tons of awards and will be sold out for months in advance. I always thought my life story would make a good musical.

Horatio: Uh…yeah…I guess that's a thing that happens?

Enter King, Queen, Laertes, Lords, Osric, and Attendants with swords and gauntlets and a table with glasses and wine.

King: We got tired of waiting, so we brought the duel to you. Okay, Hamlet, shake hands with Laertes. May the best man win. (*places Hamlet's hand in Laertes'*)

Hamlet: Listen, Laertes, I'm real sorry about earlier. I got all fired up before. I lost my cool and I feel bad, bro.

Laertes: I appreciate that man, but you disrespected me back there and I can't take that lying down, you know? (Aside) Plus there's the whole killing my dad thing. (to Hamlet) We're gonna have to duel this one out.

Hamlet: I understand. Bring the foils, it's time to duel.

Laertes: Let's do this.

Hamlet (*sarcastically*): Please, Laertes, go easy on me. I'm just a helpless lil baby compared to you.

Laertes: Are you making fun of me?

Hamlet: Me? Nooooo I would never.

V.II

King: Get these two their swords, Osric. Hamlet, do you know the bet?

Hamlet: Yes, though I think you might've bet on the wrong horse.

King: I'm not worried, I've seen how you both fight. Nobody knows dueling better than me. The odds are good. The best odds.

Laertes: This sword isn't long enough. I'm a long sword kind of guy.

Hamlet: This sword is fine for me because I'm secure in my masculinity.

Hamlet and Laertes warm up.

Osric: Okay, let's get this duel started.

King: Okay, before we get this show on the road, let's make things a little more fun. Anytime the Prince lands a blow, we'll all take a drink to his health and the trumpets will blow. Also, Laertes has to give me twenty bucks. Let's do it! Go!

Hamlet: Welp, here we go.

Laertes: Let's see what you got, you gloomy little wiener.

Hamlet and Laertes duel.

Hamlet: I got you!

Laertes: Nuh-uh!

Hamlet: Did so!

Osric: He got you, Laertes.

V.II

Trumpets blow

King: Drink up! Here you go, Hamlet, have a drink! I made it extra special for you.

Hamlet: I'm good. Let's keep going.

Hamlet and Laertes duel.

Hamlet: I got him again!

Laertes: Yeah, you got me…

King: Hamlet's looking good. He might actually win.

Queen: I don't know. He's looking a little out of breath. Hamlet, here, take Mommy's handkerchief for good luck. Whew. All this cheering is making me thirsty…

Hamlet: Thanks, Mom.

King: Uh, don't drink that, my love!

Queen: I'm sorry, I'm too dehydrated to hear you. I'm gonna take a nice long drink of this wine now. (*Drinks wine*) Hamlet, you should have some too.

King (*aside*): Hooo boyyyy. At least I'll get to get remarried again.

Hamlet: I can't right now. I need to keep my wits about me.

Queen: I love you, Hamlet! You're doing so great! I'm so proud of you!

Laertes: I'm gonna hit him now!

Hamlet: That's a weird thing to yell in the middle of a duel.

V.II

King: Do it!

Laertes: (*aside*) Although I almost feel bad about it…

Hamlet: C'mon Laertes. I've re-released the beast. Don't take it easy on me. Let's see what you got!

Laertes: Oh yeah? How about this, tough guy?

Hamlet and Laertes fight.

Osric: No blows landed!

Laertes: Take one of these!

Laertes wounds Hamlet, they grapple and end up switching swords. Then Hamlet wounds Laertes.

King: Break 'em up, break 'em up!

Hamlet: I'm not done with you, yet!

Queen falls over.

Osric: The queen is down!

Horatio: They're both bleeding! Hamlet, you okay, dude?

Osric: Are you okay, Laertes?

Laertes: Nah, he got me good. It's over for me. I'm a goner.

Hamlet: Is my mother okay?

King: Uh…she probably just fainted from the blood…

Queen (*wakes up*): Nope. Definitely not. It was the wine. Oh, my

V.II

poor baby Gus…uh…Hamlet. It was the wine. Poison! Poison!

Queen dies.

Hamlet: Lock the door! We'll find out who killed my mom!

Laertes falls over.

Laertes: Listen to me, Hamlet. You're a dead man. You're a ghost. There's nothing you can do. That sword you have in your hands? It's poisoned. I'm the one who poisoned it and I'm gonna die too. It's all the king's fault. It was all his idea.

Hamlet: The sword is poisoned? Then have a taste for yourself! (*stabs the King*)

Everyone (*shocked, gasping*): Treason, treason!

Hamlet: Adios you incestuous treasonous murderous piece of shit motherfucker. Have some more poison. (*Splashes wine in King's face*) Follow my mother. (*falls down*)

King dies.

Laertes (*weak, dying*) Yeah, he probably had that coming. (*coughs*) Listen, Hamlet, I'm real sorry about all this. I just wanted to avenge my dad. I fucked up. We cool, bro? (*holds out fist*)

Hamlet weakly fist bumps Laertes

Hamlet: I'm sorry I killed your dad. We cool.

Laertes: Sweet.

Laertes dies.

Hamlet: Horatio, dude, I'm dying here. (*to audience*) You people

(Hamlet cont.)
are just gonna sit here and watch me die? Do something! Is there a doctor in the house? Get me some anti-venom. Do some CPR! (*coughs, to Horatio*) Man, who could have seen this coming? If only someone could have warned me about this series of events killing me and everyone I love...

Horatio: (*sighs*) Yep. If only someone could have warned you... (*shakes his head*) Do you want a drink?

Hamlet: (*weak*) Yeah, I'll have a drink. Dying is thirsty work. (*drinks*) Oh Horatio. You're one of the good ones. Even if you are...ugly....and stupid ...and poor. You're one of the good ones.

Sound of canons and soldiers marching.

Hamlet: What's that?

Osric: Looks like Fortinbras coming back from Poland. I think he's giving the ambassadors from England a run for their money.

Hamlet: (*weak*) Fuck me, Horatio. This is it. I'm not even going to live to hear the news from England. What if they've figured out how to make everyone less ugly? I'd like to live to see that. Tell Fortinbras I say hi if he comes in. He was always nice to me. Okay, this is it. I'm dead. If I come back as a ghost Horatio, just...ignore me.

Hamlet dies.

Horatio: Good night sweet prince. You're sleeping with the angels now... Are the soldiers getting closer?

Enter Fortinbras and English Ambassadors and Soldiers.

Fortinbras: Haha! You've fallen for my ruse! I'm here to avenge Norway once and for all! Uh...what's going on here?

V.II

Horatio: What does it look like?

Fortinbras: It looks like…the entire Danish royal family is dead! Ah! Come on! I wanted to do that! I marched all this way for nothing? This is the worst birthday ever.

English Ambassador: Yeah, we're gonna have a problem here. We killed those two guys like the king's letter said. Now who is gonna pay us? What happened here?

Horatio: Well, as you can see, the king is…indisposed. You want to know what happened? All right, I'll tell you want happened, but sit down and grab a drink. Not that one! Pour a fresh glass. This is gonna take about…oh…two and half hours.

Fortinbras: Man…this is bullshit. I mean, I'm totally going to take over Denmark, but it sucks that the fun part is over already.

Horatio: Yeah, sure, but don't you have anything else to do?

Fortinbras: Oh, right. Uh, okay, hang on. That's Prince Hamlet there, isn't it? He was always nice to me even though I secretly hated his entire family. (*to four captains*) You four! The prince is to be buried like a solider with honors. The others are to be chopped up, deep fried, and fed to dogs. You know the drill. Take everything that isn't nailed down.

The Soldiers carry Hamlet out and start stealing stuff and moving the other bodies. As the funeral bell tolls, Horatio speaks.

Horatio: This story starts around midnight. I was standing around freezing my ass off waiting for a ghost to show up…

Fade to black, curtain.

V.II

About the Author

Photo by Erin Pearlman (Edited by Mick Theebs)

Mick Theebs is and was the first Poet Laureate of Milford, CT. In addition to desecrating famous works of literature, Mick writes poetry, fiction, and non-fiction. When he isn't writing, he enjoys hiking, cooking, and spending time with his two dogs, Yoshi and Mr. Pugsley. Yes, those are their real names.

To stay up to date with Mick's comings and goings, follow him on Twitter @MickTheebs.

www.ingramcontent.com/pod-product-compliance
Lightning Source LLC
Chambersburg PA
CBHW020910090426
42736CB00008B/567